OECD Urban Studies

Transport Bridging Divides

OECD

BETTER POLICIES FOR BETTER LIVES

This document, as well as any data and map included herein, are without prejudice to the status of or sovereignty over any territory, to the delimitation of international frontiers and boundaries and to the name of any territory, city or area.

The statistical data for Israel are supplied by and under the responsibility of the relevant Israeli authorities. The use of such data by the OECD is without prejudice to the status of the Golan Heights, East Jerusalem and Israeli settlements in the West Bank under the terms of international law.

Note by Turkey
The information in this document with reference to "Cyprus" relates to the southern part of the Island. There is no single authority representing both Turkish and Greek Cypriot people on the Island. Turkey recognises the Turkish Republic of Northern Cyprus (TRNC). Until a lasting and equitable solution is found within the context of the United Nations, Turkey shall preserve its position concerning the "Cyprus issue".

Note by all the European Union Member States of the OECD and the European Union
The Republic of Cyprus is recognised by all members of the United Nations with the exception of Turkey. The information in this document relates to the area under the effective control of the Government of the Republic of Cyprus.

Please cite this publication as:
OECD (2020), *Transport Bridging Divides*, OECD Urban Studies, OECD Publishing, Paris, *https://doi.org/10.1787/55ae1fd8-en*.

ISBN 978-92-64-74706-7 (print)
ISBN 978-92-64-57802-9 (pdf)

OECD Urban Studies
ISSN 2707-3432 (print)
ISSN 2707-3440 (online)

Foreword

The COVID-19 pandemic has had a profound impact on our daily lives. Reduced mobility has increased the up-take of digitalisation, accelerating on-going trends such as teleworking and e-commerce, raising questions about the type of transport infrastructure we have in place today – as well as the one we will need in an uncertain future.

The promise of a new vaccine provides hope of a return to normality and some degree of clarity about how the future might look. Whilst many of the changes accelerated by the pandemic are likely to remain in the 'new normal', as firms have invested in new technologies and digital infrastructures, and consumers have shifted their habits, efficient transport infrastructure remains as important today, and indeed tomorrow, as it has always been.

Much of the new normal will continue to look like the old normal: many jobs will still require physical presence, in part because many (especially personal, medical, and recreational) services will never be able to be delivered digitally. The physical connectivity of regions, producers and consumers, will remain vital to the functioning of regional and global value chains. Transport remains a crucial determinant of productivity growth, ensuring that our regions and cities remain attractive places to live and work.

However, to be effective, transport infrastructure needs to ensure equal access to opportunities such as jobs and amenities. Even before the current pandemic it was already clear that disparities existed across and within regions, with affluent areas of cities doing better, for example. The crisis has only served to exacerbate these disparities whilst also raising awareness about the importance of social cohesion and sustainable economic activity.

Transport infrastructure is a necessary requirement for economic growth but it is not sufficient on its own to close economic gaps. It is a means for development but not an end in itself, and its benefits for economic success at regional and urban level depend on the access to opportunities that it can provide.

This report addresses disparities in transport access and discusses how interregional transport infrastructure development across OECD regions contributes to economic growth, the distribution of economic activity and wider socio-economic benefits. A companion report, *OECD Urban Studies: Improving Transport Planning for Accessible Cities,* extends the analysis and provides recommendations on how transport strategies, urban planning and effective governance mechanisms can be combined to ensure inclusive and sustainable benefits from urban transport infrastructure for all.

This report was developed as part of the Programme of Work and Budget of the Regional Development Policy Committee (RDPC), supporting its agenda to promote productivity, inclusion and resilience within and across regions and cities. The project benefited from the financial support from the European Commission's Directorate-General for Regional and Urban Policy (DG REGIO) as part of a wider project on *Rethinking urban and regional transport needs: improving access, safety and well-being through transport investment and policies.*

Acknowledgements

This report was produced by the OECD Centre for Entrepreneurship, SMEs, Regions and Cities (CFE) led by Lamia Kamal-Chaoui, Director. It is part of the Programme of Work of the OECD's Regional Development Policy Committee (RDPC).

The report is the outcome of a joint project by CFE and the OECD's International Transport Forum (ITF). The financial contributions by the European Commission's Directorate-General for Regional and Urban Policy, as well as the support and feedback received at various stages of the project by Lewis Dijkstra are gratefully acknowledged.

The OECD Secretariat would particularly like to thank Martin Adler, Or Levkovich and Ilias Pasidis, as well as Neil Lee for the preparation of two background papers that underpin this report and Dimitrios Papaioannou of the ITF who provided data, comments and support for the analysis based on the EC-ITF-OECD Urban Access Framework. The OECD Secretariat would also like to thank the numerous local officials and experts that provided valuable insights during the case study missions in Madrid, Prague, Romania and Vancouver - in particular, Andrew Devlin, Andrew McCurran and Kyle Rosenke from TransLink and Heather McNell and James Stiver from Metro Vancouver (Canada), Laura Delgado Fernández and Francisco Javier López Gómez from the Consorcio Regional de Transportes de Madrid (Spain), Jaromír Hainc and Kristina Kleinwachterová from the Prague Institute of Planning and Development (Czech Republic), and Liviu Băileșteanu and Radu Necsuliu from the Ministry of Regional Development of Romania for their kind assistance in organising the study missions and providing valuable information for the report and case studies.

The project and publication were coordinated by Alexander C. Lembcke under the supervision of Rudiger Ahrend, Head of Division: Economic Analysis, Statistics and Multi-level Governance in CFE. The report was prepared by Federica Daniele with contributions by Oscar Huerta Melchor and Alexander C. Lembcke. Oscar Huerta Melchor coordinated four case studies in three cities Madrid (Spain), Prague (Czech Republic) and Vancouver (Canada) and in Romania's Central and West regions that include contributions by Jared Gars and Antonio Canamas Catala. Abel Schumann provided additional input for the report. Charles Victor and Jeanette Duboys provided administrative support throughout the project's implementation phase.

This report was submitted to RDPC Delegates for approval by written procedure by 27 November 2020 under the cote CFE/RDPC(2020)20. The final version was edited and formatted by Eleonore Morena and received editorial input from Alexandra Taylor. Pilar Philip prepared the manuscript for publication.

Table of contents

Tables

Figures

Boxes

Follow OECD Publications on:

http://twitter.com/OECD_Pubs

http://www.facebook.com/OECDPublications

http://www.linkedin.com/groups/OECD-Publications-4645871

http://www.youtube.com/oecdilibrary

http://www.oecd.org/oecddirect/

Executive summary

Transport infrastructure connects businesses, people and places. It provides firms with access to markets, workers with access to jobs and cities and regions with access to the global economy. Transport infrastructure has been a necessary condition for economic development for centuries and remains an important factor in the catching up of economically weaker regions. Public investment reflects its importance. In many OECD member countries, total inland transport infrastructure investment, i.e. investment in road and rail, amounts to more than 1% of gross domestic product (GDP), not even accounting for maintenance spending for the existing stock.

Transport bridging economic divides

Improving transport networks yield both an immediate as well as a delayed economic dividend for regions. Through better integration into the wider transport network, regions immediately gain greater accessibility, i.e. greater market access. For incumbent firms this means that they can reach more consumers for the same cost of transport, thereby increasing their potential customer or client base. Such an increase in their market allows firms to scale up production and leverage efficiency gains. Areas with better accessibility provide stronger incentives for new and existing firms to locate there. Better access means firms can take advantage of the cheaper cost of land and rent, without foregoing a suitably deep pool of workers. A delayed dividend accrues over time. As other regions grow, the market that can be reached from a connected region increases as well. Both dividends matter in practice. For access to people (population in regions), two-thirds of the improvements in European regions between 1990 and 2012 came from the construction of new highways, and one-third from population growth in already connected regions. For GDP, a more dynamic factor, new highways contributed only 20% of market access improvements, while growth in already connected regions contributed 80%.

Economic benefits from greater accessibility are sizeable for all types of regions. A 10% improvement in market access increases GDP in a region by 2%, on average. To put this into perspective, market access in the French Haute-Garonne region and its main city Toulouse increased by 40% between 1990 and 2012, resulting in an 8% increase in GDP. There are, however, limits to economic gains that transport infrastructure can provide as today's well-developed highway network provides a high degree of accessibility in many parts of continental Europe. Nevertheless, there are still places, where benefits from improvements in accessibility can be substantial, especially in Eastern Europe.

Transport investment cannot bridge all regional divides. Transport infrastructure investment may amplify or create differences in the economic trajectory of regions. A study for Spain, for example, finds that after the opening of a new motorway, municipalities within 10 km had, on average, more than 13 percentage points higher firm creation rates than those 10-20 km away. Investment decisions therefore entail important choices in terms of location, path and timing of construction of new infrastructures. Decisions should be taken after careful deliberation of the potential local and aggregate gains and losses, using careful cost-benefit analyses in line with best practices in the OECD.

Transport bridging urban divides

Accessibility improvements in urban transport raise productivity and wages but also housing costs. Firms and workers in larger cities are more productive due to "agglomeration benefits", i.e. economic gains related to density. These benefits arise in large part through more opportunities for formal and informal interaction and learning for people, including a greater variety of jobs that match workers' skills. The results are higher wages for workers but also higher housing costs as neighbourhoods with greater access are coveted by an increasing number of people. At the same time, residents in each neighbourhood can only access a limited number of opportunities at reasonable travel distance. For residents living outside the city centre the number of opportunities is often much more limited compared to the total opportunities in the metropolitan area. Accessibility depends on the speed and efficiency of the transport system but also on how far people have to travel to reach their destination. To boost accessibility a city has therefore two options: it can target improvements in the performance of a particular transport mode or bring its population and their destinations closer together, for example by providing more opportunities where people live.

Larger cities offer residents access to more opportunities but those living in the commuting zone generally require a car. Within a 30-minute ride using public transport, residents in Europe's larger metropolitan areas (more than 2 million inhabitants) can access about 3 times as many shops – taken as a proxy of access to opportunities – as residents in Europe's smaller metropolitan areas (400 000 to 750 000 inhabitants). Public transport provides access within the city centre itself, while residents of the commuting zone typically have to rely on their car to reach a sizeable variety of shops. Even when travelling by car, the degree of access differs between the commuting zone and the city centre. In the metropolitan area of Rome, Italy's capital city, the average resident living in the commuting zone can reach about 390 shops by driving 30 minutes. In comparison, a resident of Rome's dense urban centre can reach more than 2 400 shops by car and more than 1 500 shops within 30 minutes using public transport.

Transport investment needs complementary policies to be effective at improving accessibility for everyone. In large metropolitan areas, better accessibility is to a significant extent driven by greater proximity (i.e. shorter distances) to opportunities. Greater density reduces travel times, with the latter making for more attractive cities. For metropolitan areas with fewer than 750 000 inhabitants, however, proximity matters less than the efficiency of the transport system in providing access to opportunities. Investment to improve the efficiency of the transport system can raise accessibility in a neighbourhood but is unlikely to translate into better accessibility for low-income residents without additional measures. Even if investment targets less affluent neighbourhoods, prices for housing and rents in those neighbourhoods will rise alongside accessibility improvements. Complementary policies such as increased housing supply through the densification around transport links or dedicated affordable housing can alleviate these cost pressures. Additional policies can focus on bringing opportunities to people living in low-income neighbourhoods by favouring mixed land-use to increase the proximity between people and opportunities.

Transport moving regions and cities forward

Ageing, the transition towards climate-neutral economies, the sharing economy and not least the current COVID-19 pandemic require rethinking the future of transport. An important trend was the gradual shift in investment priorities from road to less carbon-emitting rail, with inland infrastructure investment dedicated to rail increasing from 28% in 2000 to 31% in 2016 across OECD member countries. COVID-19 has driven people back into their cars. Rebuilding engagement with public transport will thus be crucial in the months to come. There are also opportunities arising from the pandemic, particularly in cities. At least 150 cities around the world have created temporary bicycle lanes and other spaces for active transport, taking back roads from cars.

1 Transport infrastructure trends and regional development

This chapter provides an overview of recent trends on transport infrastructure development in European and OECD member countries and reviews the main benefits associated with it. It starts with a description of how transport infrastructure investment has changed across countries and regions, both in terms of the magnitude and its composition, paying particular attention to differences between urban and rural regions. Next, it moves onto reviewing the main benefits associated with an efficient transport system, all while making suggestions on how current evaluation tools, such as cost-benefit analysis, could be improved to account for all of them. It emphasises the need for different metrics that can better capture the potential of transport infrastructure improvements and the importance of taking a "more aggregate" view when evaluating investment projects that can account for potential displacement of economic activity. The main benefits are discussed in reference to the type of investment: interregional highway and railway – both traditional and high-speed – development, highway development in the proximity of cities and infrastructure development within cities.

Transport infrastructure was, is and will be important for regional development

Transport infrastructure and economic development

Extensive and efficient transport infrastructure is essential for well-functioning economies and the development of regions and cities. When designed effectively, transport networks can be an engine for productivity and improved quality of life for citizens. "Effective modes of transport – including high-quality roads, railroads, ports, and air transport – enable entrepreneurs to get their goods and services to market in a secure and timely manner and facilitate the movement of workers to the most suitable jobs" (World Economic Forum, 2016, p. 35[1]). For instance, Chile has rolled-out many key investments in its basic infrastructure backbone that are essential for economic development and welfare. This has led to improvements in living standards and Chile's gross domestic product (GDP) per capita has increased from USD 4 787 in 1990 to USD 22 197 in 2015 (OECD, 2017[2]).

Transport infrastructure investment has always been a fundamental engine of economic development. The facilitating role of transport infrastructure with respect to trade for instance can be traced back in history. A producer in New York in the late 18th century was bound to sell primarily to consumers on the East Coast of the United States. However, less than a century later the same producer had the opportunity to sell to a consumer living in Los Angeles thanks to the railroad network built in the United States between 1790 and 1870.[1]

Transport infrastructure investment creates economic growth through many different channels. The most basic among them is that transport infrastructure facilitates the exchange of goods. Improved transport infrastructure reduces the cost of trade. Better domestic trade opportunities allow regions to specialise in the sector where they are the most competitive relative to the others. This holds irrespective of the type of regional economy, be it more urban or rural. Beyond the domestic borders, better foreign trade opportunities can unlock not just regional but even countrywide export-driven economic growth. This creates benefits for the exporting firms within a region but also wider benefits if the exported good is integrated into local, regional or global value chains.

Transport infrastructure allows regions and cities to leverage benefits from agglomeration and concentration by expanding commuting opportunities for their workers. This creates benefits for places and for workers who can access better-matching and better-paid jobs without bearing the burden of moving to a different place. Intra-urban and suburban transport infrastructure serves to integrate rural regions into the local labour market of the cities located in their proximity, thereby creating a greater variety in job opportunities and raising the living standards of their inhabitants. For instance, in 1990, the average commute in Korea was less than ten kilometres. Following a round of investment in transport infrastructure, 20 years later, this distance had increased by 30% to 13 kilometres while the time an average Korean worker spent commuting decreased by about one-quarter (OECD, 2016[3]). Similarly, the number of daily commuters between the southern Swedish region of Skåne and Copenhagen in Denmark rose roughly sevenfold to around 20 000 per day after the opening in 2000 of the Øresund bridge (OECD, 2016[4]). Beyond commuting, distances that can be travelled in 2-3 hours allow for business-related day trips that can enhance business interactions, in particular between urban centres. Since 1994, close to 430 million passengers have crossed the Channel tunnel connecting London in the United Kingdom to Paris in France across all transport modes (e.g. the Eurostar train or the Eurotunnel Shuttles) (GETLINK, 2019[5]).[2]

Transport infrastructure brings firms closer to a larger customer base and a larger pool of workers, which can stimulate hiring and investment by local firms. For instance, a firm that gains access to a broader market thanks to the reduction in transport costs that accompanies improved transport infrastructure might decide to invest more resources to enhance its competitiveness. Alternatively, a firm facing an increase in demand might choose to tap into its unutilised capacity and hire more local workers in order to serve an expanding market. An increase in production will cause an increase in the density of local economic activity further reinforced by productivity spill-overs among neighbouring firms.[3]

Investing in transport infrastructure

In general, OECD member countries have substantial needs for new investment in transport infrastructure as well as upgrading existing infrastructure. Governments increasingly face tough decisions about where to locate or maintain public investments as resources become scarcer and investment needs multiply. It is increasingly important that service and policy restructuring decisions reflect the diversity of needs and circumstances facing urban and rural communities, and try to maximise the value for money that investment can provide in each context. However, the quality of existing public infrastructure has deteriorated and public infrastructure stock has started to drop in many European countries (CEB, 2017[6]).

Transport infrastructure investment remains one of the key decisions taken by policymakers and accounts for a large fraction of OECD countries' budgets. In 2016, the average total inland transport infrastructure investment amounted to roughly 1% of GDP across member countries of the OECD International Transport Forum (ITF) (Figure 1.1).[4] Transport infrastructure investment peaks during times of major transport infrastructure project execution, this being one of the reasons behind the dispersion in the 2000-16 difference in transport infrastructure investment (as a percentage of GDP). There are other potential reasons, e.g. the change in construction cost. In the United States, for instance, state spending per kilometre rose fivefold between 1960 and 1980 during the construction of Interstate Highways, the most significant infrastructure network in the United States. Increasing demand for transport infrastructure as income levels rose accounts for a large part of that increase (Brooks and Liscow, 2019[7]). Another reason behind the variation in spending as a percentage of GDP is, of course, fluctuation in GDP. For instance, Greece registered a high positive variation in transport infrastructure investment as a percentage of GDP during 2000-16, primarily because its GDP contracted substantially over the same period.

Figure 1.1. Total inland transport infrastructure investment as a percentage of GDP, 2000 and 2016

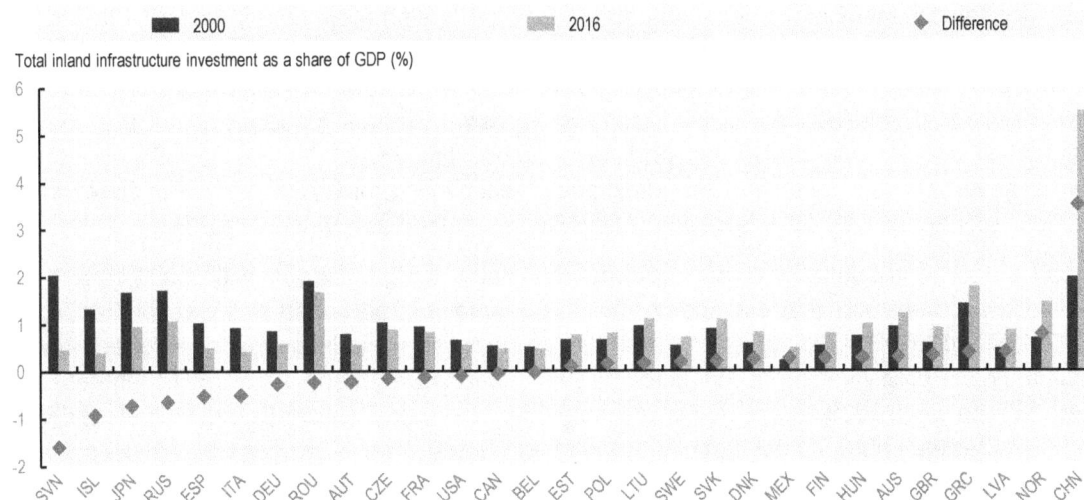

Note: Countries are sorted in ascending order of the difference in the share of total infrastructure investment over GDP between 2000 and 2016.
Source: ITF (2019[8]), ITF Transport Infrastructure Database, https://doi.org/10.1787/trsprt-data-en (accessed on 29 July 2019).

Large infrastructural projects continue in both the developed and the developing world. Some examples are the Trans-European Transport Network in Europe (Box 1.2), to the Golden Quadrilateral in India and Interoceanic Highway in South America. The government of the People's Republic of China (China hereafter) has been leading a global development strategy, the Belt and Road Initiative, consisting of several transport infrastructure projects with the ambition to connect 65 countries representing over 30% of world GDP (World Bank, 2018[9]).

Transport infrastructure investment is not the only source of spending on transport infrastructure. Countries spend a large amount of money every year on maintaining it. For 11 of the 26 OECD member countries with available data, maintenance spending for inland transport infrastructure was again half the amount spent on infrastructure investment in 2016. For Italy, Latvia and Slovenia, maintenance spending even exceeded investment.[5]

Large infrastructural projects require buy-in from a large number of national and regional partners. This is the case for the abovementioned Belt and Road Initiative, as well as for the European Transport Network, where a large share of spending takes place at the supranational level. For instance, during the 2014-20 programming period, about 22% of the European Regional and Development Fund (ERDF) and the Cohesion Fund is being invested in network infrastructure in transport and energy.[6]

Transport infrastructure investment has been severely hit by the Great Recession thus leading to the emergence of significant funding gaps. Transport infrastructure spending still accounts for a significant share of countries' budgets but the current trajectory points to a shortfall of about USD 350 billion a year (excluding spending due to maintenance backlogs), a gap that triples after considering the extent of transport infrastructure investment needed to meet the United Nations (UN) Sustainable Development Goals (McKinsey & Company, 2016[10]). As countries are looking for strategies to bolster their economies following the ongoing COVID-19 pandemic, transport investment provides an opportunity to move towards greening cities. Investment in electric vehicle charging infrastructure is a key opportunity for recovery packages, both for private vehicles and electrified public transport such as buses (OECD, 2020[11]).

Transport infrastructure, particularly public transport, are delivered and used at the local level. For instance, across Europe, between 2009 and 2015, local and state (regional) governments represented on average 53.6% of total public capital investment (CEB, 2017[6]). The level of investment depends on the type of infrastructure. According to the CEB (2017[6]), subnational governments in Europe tend to invest more in social infrastructure (education, health and community services). In economic infrastructure (transport, amenities and telecommunication), local and state (regional) government contributed 37.1% and central government 62.9% of total investment (CEB, 2017[6]). In OECD countries, subnational governments represented on average 59.3% of total public investment and 3.1% of GDP (Allain-Dupré, Hulbert and Vincent, 2017[12]). There are certainly variations across countries depending on their levels of decentralisation and political system. In particular, across the OECD, 39.2% of total investment by subnational governments is located to economic affairs, accounting for 0.73% of GDP in 2014 where the single most important item by far is transport (Allain-Dupré, Hulbert and Vincent, 2017[12]).

There was a decline in subnational infrastructure investment across European Union (EU) and OECD countries following the global financial crisis of 2007-08 (Allain-Dupré, Hulbert and Vincent, 2017[12]; CEB, 2017[6]). According to OECD studies, the decline in subnational public investment has been particularly marked in the EU. Public investment conducted by subnational governments across EU countries dropped by almost 18% between 2009 and 2014 (i.e. 5% per year in real terms) (Allain-Dupré, Hulbert and Vincent, 2017[12]). The decline varies across countries and regions, and sectors. In general, between 2010 and 2015, economic affairs (where transport infrastructure is the most important component) has been largely spared by investment cuts as capital expenditures remain almost stable in real terms. However, subnational transport investments declined in Greece, Ireland, Italy, Lithuania and Spain. By contrast, subnational government investment in transport has been rising in Scandinavian countries and in Central European countries that benefit from EU structural and cohesion funds (Allain-Dupré, Hulbert and Vincent, 2017[12]).

Underinvestment in transport infrastructure across regions and cities could limit the possibilities of economic growth and social development. In the United States, for instance, public transport is an important factor in the Chicago Tri-State Metro Region's attractiveness but investment in the system has not kept up with the needs of a suburbanising population, which has led to road congestion and emissions (OECD, 2012[13]). Governance is an important factor limiting the effectiveness of public transport in the metropolitan area, as fragmentation leads to challenges associated with a lack of interconnectivity, coherence across transit modes, regional freight planning, accountability, and implementation power for regional planning and transport objectives (OECD, 2015[14]). More broadly, investing in the construction and upgrading of transport infrastructure could help to improve the connectivity between rural and urban areas and boost local economies. However, according to some studies, there has been a long-term decline in the availability of infrastructure as the stock of public capital (closely related to infrastructure) as a share of output has fallen over the last three decades across the world (IMF, 2014[15]). The impact of the global financial crisis of 2007-08 has been deep and investment in infrastructure remains below pre-crisis levels in many countries (UNECE, 2016[16]; Allain-Dupré, Hulbert and Vincent, 2017[12]). To support investment in infrastructure, governments may have to prioritise subsectors where infrastructure is the poorest (i.e. the railway sector in Romania and the road sector in Ukraine). Returns on infrastructure investment are higher where current endowments are lower (UNECE, 2016[16]).

Current and future challenges in transport investment

Gains from transport infrastructure investment in some regions might be offset by losses in other regions. The construction of the National Trunk Highway System in China, for example, helped connected urban prefectures to become more attractive, whereas rural prefectures shrank in size (Baum-Snow et al., 2016[17]). From a public policy perspective, this means that any assessment of the overall benefits of transport infrastructure needs to account for trade-offs and displacement. This section provides a broader description of the benefits of road and rail infrastructure and the potential negative externalities imposed on other regions by transport infrastructure investment in one region.

Current megatrends – demographic transition, climate change, digitalisation and automation – are creating additional pressures on transport networks (OECD, 2019[18]). The demand for transport infrastructure is expected to rise in response to increasing urbanisation rates.[7] Supply of transport infrastructure will need to keep pace if urbanisation is to take place without a slowdown in economic growth or a loss in living standards.[8] Even the current COVID-19 pandemic is unlikely to reverse mounting pressures. Public transport networks play a crucial role in helping cities adapt to megatrends. As the lockdowns across OECD member countries relaxed following the first wave of infections, travel resumed quickly but public transport use remained (significantly) below pre-crisis levels, e.g. in London, there was less than half the number of daily riders on the underground on every single day between April and October 2020 than during comparable days in prior years.[9] Increased teleworking accounts for part of this decline but a relative shift towards other individual modes of transport is also evident.

Future investment in transport infrastructure must address concerns about environmental sustainability. As countries are starting to commit to net-zero carbon emissions, an increasing number of green and innovative mobility solutions are becoming available and need to be integrated into transport planning. It might even be necessary to completely rethink and redesign mobility systems around accessibility (OECD, 2019[19]).

Technological change implies a redefinition of infrastructure investment needs. On the one hand, digitalisation of society demands investments in broadband infrastructure and the expansion of data centres capacity. Estimates by the European Commission (EC) and the European Investment Bank (EIB) suggest that additional investment worth approximately EUR 55 million a year is required to meet the targets of the EU digital agenda (European Parliament Research Service, 2018[20]). On the other hand, the changing landscape of urban mobility implies the need to convert existing infrastructure, e.g. parking space.

Better data can help steer policy decisions. For example, the use of high capacity vehicles for freight traffic should be encouraged in light of the data that the information and communication technology (ICT) on board these vehicles make it possible to collect. High capacity vehicles are freight trucks that are heavier or longer (or both) than vehicles currently permitted on the general road network. It is estimated that the costs of adapting the existing highway network to the circulation of such vehicles are modest especially when compared to the benefits in terms of reduction of the cost of moving goods and energy demand. Most importantly, these vehicles usually come equipped with in-vehicle sensors that, matched with road-sensors, allow the collection of real-time and fine-grained tracking data that can be used as inputs in traffic management systems seeking to reduce traffic and carbon emissions (ITF, 2019[21]).

The benefits of transport infrastructure investments may increasingly accrue through complementarities and synergies among a cluster of assets rather than stand-alone projects. Such complementarities are easier to find and match at the regional and local levels. With many of the large infrastructures complete, future transport investments will involve extensions to or linkages with other existing infrastructures. Intermodality would need to be further promoted as it could facilitate the movement of goods and people across transport modes and developing the so-called "last mile" infrastructure. This requires better co-ordination at the planning phase and complex interactions at the implementation stage.

To improve the actual access to opportunities that transport infrastructure can provide, it is necessary to increase the investment in transit to increase travel capacity. Transit is a set of technologies (trains, underground, light rail, bus rapid transit and regular buses) that differs from private means of transport. Increasing travel capacity has high fixed costs and they become more advantageous at a high enough population density; thus, investments have to be strategic. For instance, the high costs of the metro systems relative to buses make metros attractive only for the parts of the city with a sufficiently high population density. Moreover, the experience of developed and developing cities shows that fostering accessibility is more than increasing travel capacity and investing in transit technologies. It is a combination of urban policies aimed at easing access to destinations without having necessarily to use public transport and at a low travel cost (Duranton and Guerra, 2016[22]). As the experience of London suggests, every city and every part of the city is unique and requires tailored transport solutions to support growth and socio-economic development (Greater London Authority, 2018[23]).

Solid evidence and evaluation are crucial to tackling the challenges policymakers face when taking transport investment decision. This might require rethinking traditional *ex ante* evaluation methods such as cost-benefit analysis (CBA), by adopting more comprehensive evaluation criteria to assess the admissibility of potential transport infrastructure projects as a function of their policy objectives (Box 1.1). For instance, a quantitative assessment of the impact of transport infrastructure investment on employment and productivity at different geographical scales is often beyond the scope of standard CBA, which is currently the most widely adopted evaluation tool of transport infrastructure projects.[10] The list of costs considered in a CBA can also be expanded depending on the policy objective of the project. For instance, given that transport infrastructure investment can disproportionately benefit high-income households, the increase in inequality should be added to the costs of the project if one of its implicit goals is to ensure that the benefits are more equally distributed among the population.

Box 1.1. Externalities and cost-benefit analysis

Among the channels that tools such as CBA traditionally consider are the "cash in-flows directly paid by users for the goods or services provided by the operation, such as charges borne directly by users for the use of infrastructure, sale or rent of land or buildings, or payments for services" (EC, 2014[24]). For example, the price charged for a train ticket is among the revenues and therefore benefits associated with rail investment. Benefits typically accounted for in CBA can also be non-financial, such as savings in travel time, the reduced cost of accidents and environmental externalities.

Despite the long list of channels already accounted for, CBA can gain from the inclusion of further benefits. For example, the impact that transport infrastructure investment has on capital investment, employment or productivity in the regions connected to new infrastructures. The upcoming section provides a more detailed discussion of these benefits. CBA should also account for externalities that investment creates beyond directly connected places. This is because transport infrastructure investment does not just have an impact on the regions it crosses but one that often extends onto neighbouring regions. Moreover, positive consequences for one region can also come at the expense of others (Baum-Snow et al., 2016[17]). Hence, in the end, whether there is an aggregate net gain depends on the individual case.

Source: EC (2014[24]), *Guide to Cost-Benefit Analysis of Investment Projects*, European Commission; Baum-Snow, N. et al. (2016[17]), "Highways, market access, and urban growth in China".

Investing in quality and maintenance

There are marked differences in the availability and quality of infrastructure across countries but differences are being bridged. For instance, in the EU, the new member states have been catching up with older members (UNECE, 2016[16]). However, the perception of the quality of infrastructure remains very low in many of those countries. According to the *Global Competitiveness Report*'s Executive Opinion Survey, in OECD member countries in general, the perceived quality of railroad infrastructure (4.4 out of 7) is relatively lower to that of road infrastructure (5 out of 7) (Figure 1.2). This suggests that roads are more reliable than railroads. France and Japan are the two OECD countries ranked among the top three of high-quality perception of both roads and railroad infrastructure. The perception of the quality of road infrastructure in countries such as Austria, Belgium, Mexico, New Zealand and Norway is lower than the OECD average. Meanwhile, Japan and Switzerland have the highest quality perception of railroad infrastructure.

The road and railroad networks are two important subsectors of the transport network. Investment in their expansion and maintenance is critical. The sheer size of many transport networks has made them increasingly costlier to maintain. Many countries have accumulated very large gaps in the required maintenance work to their transport infrastructure network so that maintenance backlogs will absorb a considerable amount of resources invested in transport infrastructure (McKinsey & Company, 2016[10]). When roads do not meet quality standards the average speed decreases and the safety is compromised. For instance, in Ukraine, where road quality perception is rather low, the speed on highways is one-third to one-half of what it is in Western Europe; and fatality rates per 100 000 inhabitants reached 11.3 in 2013, well above the OECD average of 6.8 (OECD, 2018[25]). In Romania, the road network is of major importance for local and regional development. However, although the road network covers the entire network of communes and cities, the road infrastructure is of poor quality and needs extensive maintenance and upgrading. For instance, in the central region, of the 4 696 km of county roads, only 42% have electricity and 33% are cobbled or dirt roads. Moreover, there are over 4 000 km of communal roads that connect the centre and villages. However, only 10% have light duty coating and half of it is outdated; in addition, 80% of communal roads are cobbled or dirt roads.

In many countries, the railway system is the backbone of long-distance freight transport. Underinvestment in railways could represent significant setbacks for economic development. In some East European countries, railway infrastructure requires considerable modernisation. Also, freight shipments use the same rail line, decreasing considerably the average speed of passenger trains; and the average age of locomotives and passenger cars is above 40 years. In Romania, the railway infrastructure suffers from deterioration and the railway fleet is obsolete and inadequate to meet current requirements. For example, at the national level, 4 000 km of railway (30% of the network) have been in need of rehabilitation for more than a decade. This has led to an increase in dangerous points and 44% increase in the length of the railway network affected by speed restrictions, to the detriment of the quality of the services offered. The average travel speed value achieved by passenger trains, taking into account standing at stations, is between 28-58 km/h. For express trains, the average speed is only 20 km/h higher. The low quality of railroad infrastructure means that most of the freight is done by road, which in many cases are secondary congested roads.

Figure 1.2. Quality of road and railway infrastructure

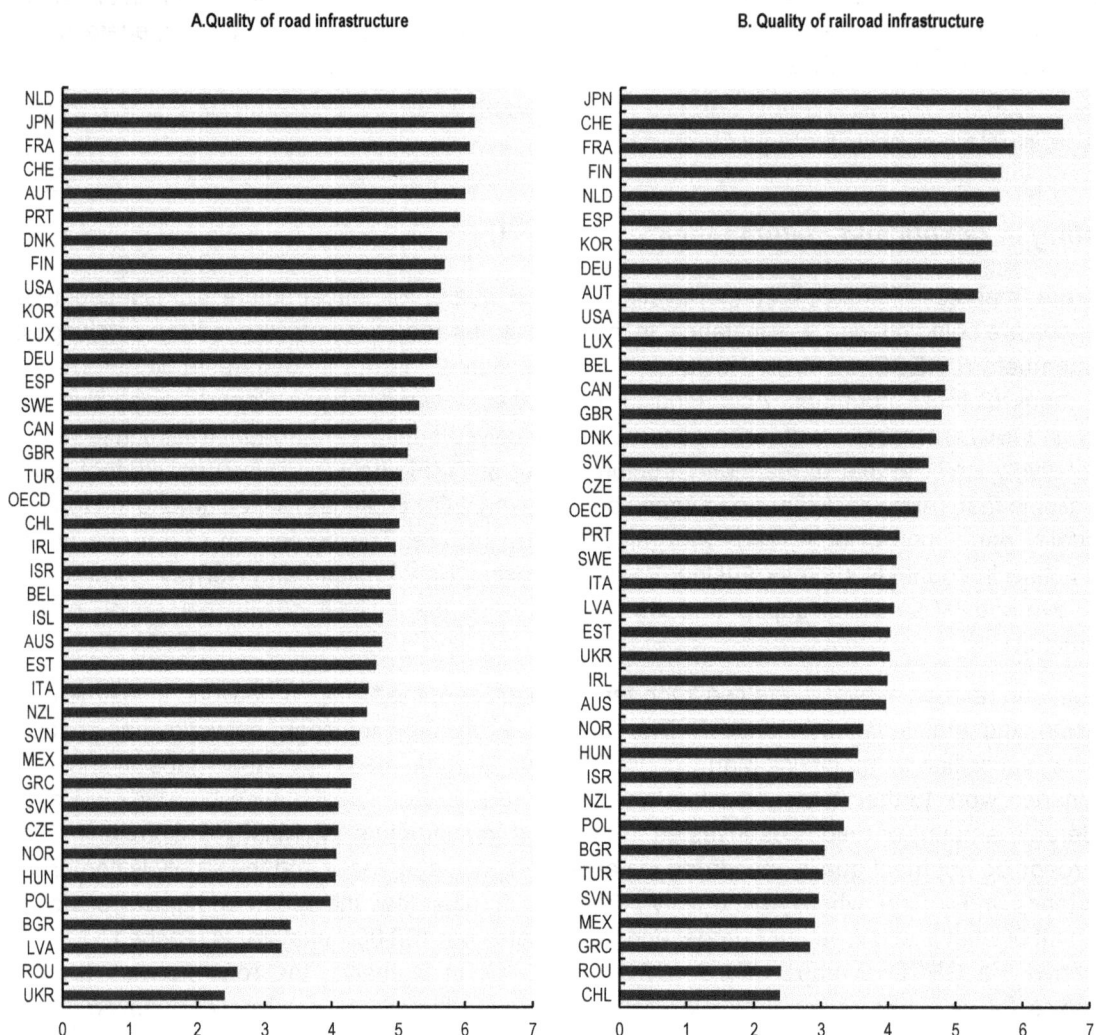

A.Quality of road infrastructure   B. Quality of railroad infrastructure

Note: *The Global Competitiveness Report*'s Executive Opinion Survey asks business executives to evaluate, on a scale from 1 to 7, one particular aspect of their operating environment (in this case the quality – extensiveness and condition – of road and railroad infrastructure). Source: Prepared based on World Economic Forum (2016[1]), *The Global Competitiveness Report 2016-2017*, http://www3.weforum.org/docs/GCR2016-2017/05FullReport/TheGlobalCompetitivenessReport2016-2017_FINAL.pdf (accessed on 5 September 2019); published in OECD (2018[25]), *Maintaining the Momentum of Decentralisation in Ukraine*, https://dx.doi.org/10.1787/9789264301436-en.

Shifting priorities and catching up in transport infrastructure investment

Trends in transport infrastructure investment

Investment in road and rail infrastructure has increased in many countries. In 2016, total inland transport infrastructure investment as a share of GDP was higher than in 2000 in half of the countries for which data are available. For most countries, investment increased to drive this expansion. For instance, the United Kingdom, total inland transport infrastructure investment nearly doubled between 2000 and 2016, despite GDP growth of 33% over the whole period. There are exceptions: in Greece, the increase in investment intensity came through a contraction in GDP between 2000 and 2016.

The composition of total inland transport infrastructure investment changed between 2000 and 2016, shifting towards rail investment. In 2000, the share of total transport infrastructure investment on roads across 18 countries was 62% while, in 2016, this figure was down to 58%. At the same time, the share in railway investment has increased from 28% to 31%. The shift has been quite heterogeneous among countries: while France raised its share of rail investment by 26 percentage points, Poland saw it contracting by 6 percentage points. Overall, the increase in rail investment was driven by Western European countries, while East European ones saw an expansion in total inland infrastructure investment driven primarily by road investment. These differential trends between East and Western European countries should also be interpreted in light of the different starting points, and the need for East European countries to catch up with average road length in the rest of Europe (Figure 1.3).

Figure 1.3. Shares of total inland transport infrastructure investment by transport mode

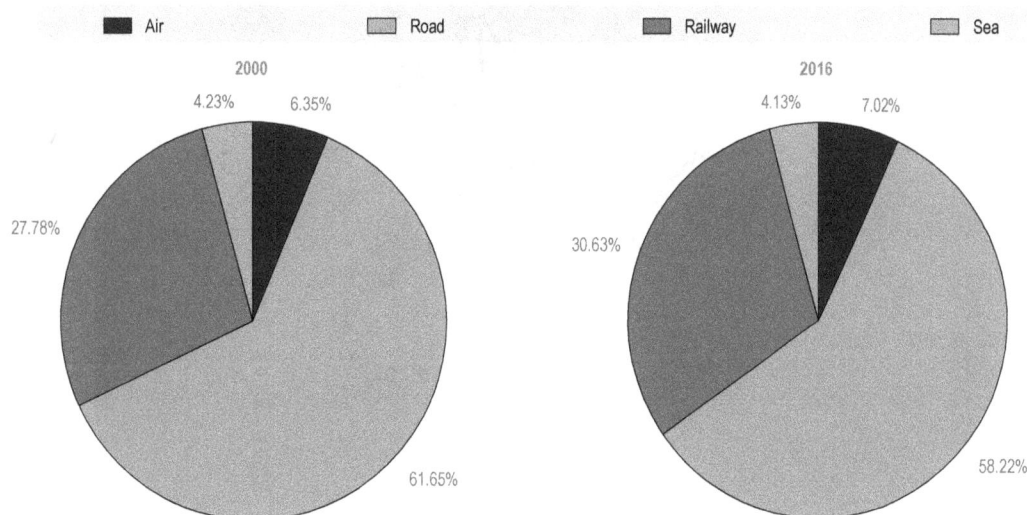

Note: Data for BEL, CAN, DNK, EST, FIN, FRA, DEU, GRC, ITA, LTU, LUX, MEX, NOR, POL, PRT, SVN, ESP. For countries for which the year 2016 is not available, the most recent available year is used: DNK (2015), LUX (2015), PRT (2014), POL (2013).
Source: ITF (2019[8]), *ITF Transport Infrastructure Database*, https://doi.org/10.1787/trsprt-data-en (accessed on 29 July 2019).

The shift towards railway spending in the past two decades occurred alongside additional highway investment. The European highway network expanded considerably between 1990 and 2012 (Figure 1.4). The highway network is part of the road network that comprises also motorways, secondary or regional roads. In some countries, the expansion in the highway network was mostly completed well before the 2000s: for example, most of the expansion in the Spanish highway network took place in the early 1990s. In others, especially the East European countries, the development of the highway network started later and it is still underway.

Figure 1.4. The highway network in Europe in 1990 (black lines) and 2012 (red lines)

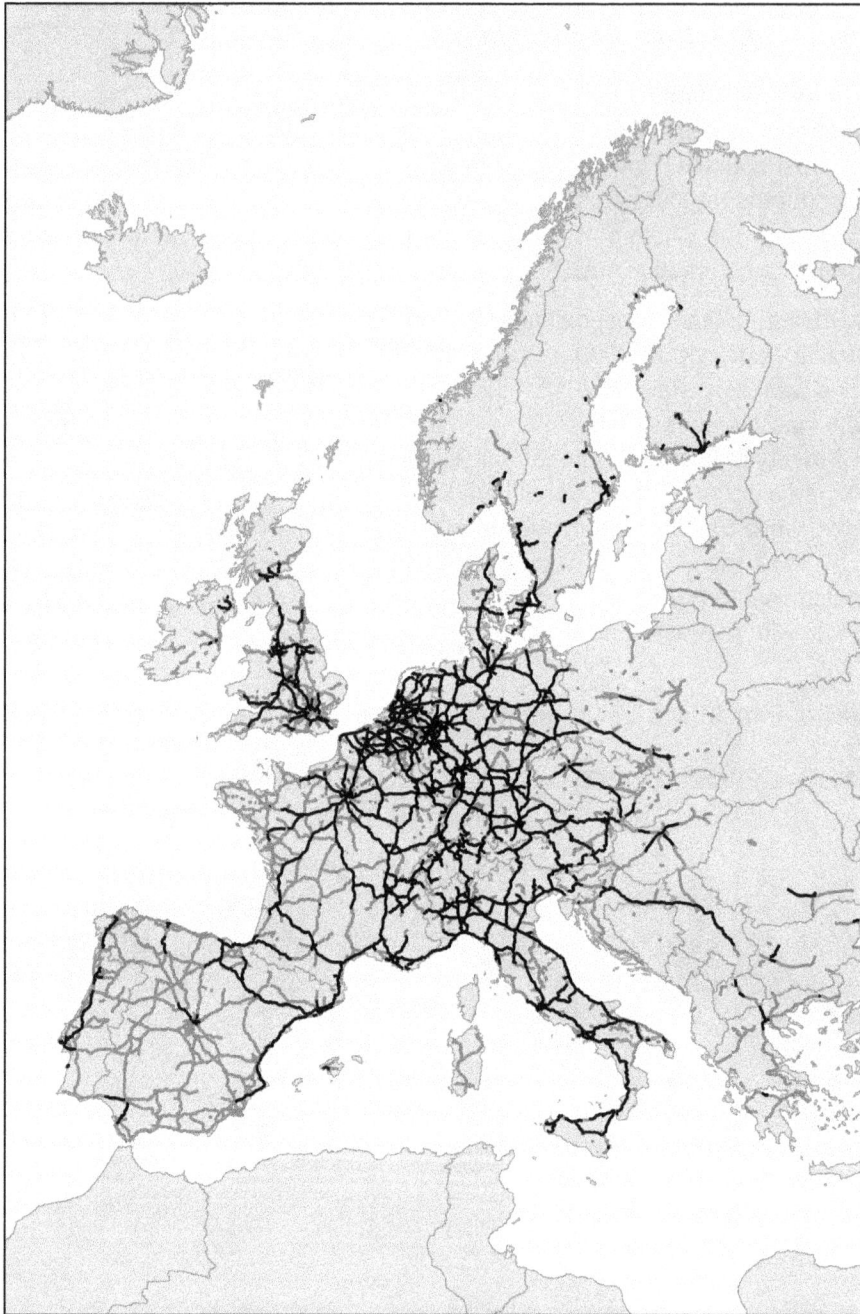

Source: Based on Stelder, D. (2016[26]), "Regional accessibility trends in Europe: Road infrastructure, 1957-2012", *Regional Studies*, Vol. 50/6, pp. 983-995.

From road to rail

Between 2000 and 2014, the level of per capita CO_2 emissions grew less in countries with higher per capita investment in inland transport infrastructure (Figure 1.5). This might seem counterintuitive since transport accounts for 30% of CO_2 emissions in OECD member countries (ITF, 2019[27]). Part of the explanation is the fact that countries that invested more resources in inland transport infrastructure and also expanded their share of rail investment between 2000 and 2014. The railway is in fact among the most energy-efficient and lowest-emitting transport modes (IEA, 2019[28]).

The COVID-19 crisis has left rail operators in financial trouble. As lockdown measures restricted interregional and international travel, railway companies saw demand drop dramatically. In Canada, domestic and international rail passengers in April 2020 were less than 2% of the number of passengers in April 2019.[11] By July 2020, the number of passengers had risen again but remained at only about 16% of the passenger volume in July 2019. Even in Sweden, one of the countries with the least stringent lockdown restrictions, passenger volumes on trains were 20% or more below the prior year between March and June 2020, and about 10% lower since then.[12] To buffer the shock on their rail sectors, OECD countries have taken steps early in the pandemic to ensure companies remain functional, spending billions in bailouts or absorbing losses in their balance sheets (where operators are already public).

Figure 1.5. Inland infrastructure investment, rail investment and CO_2 emissions, 2000-14

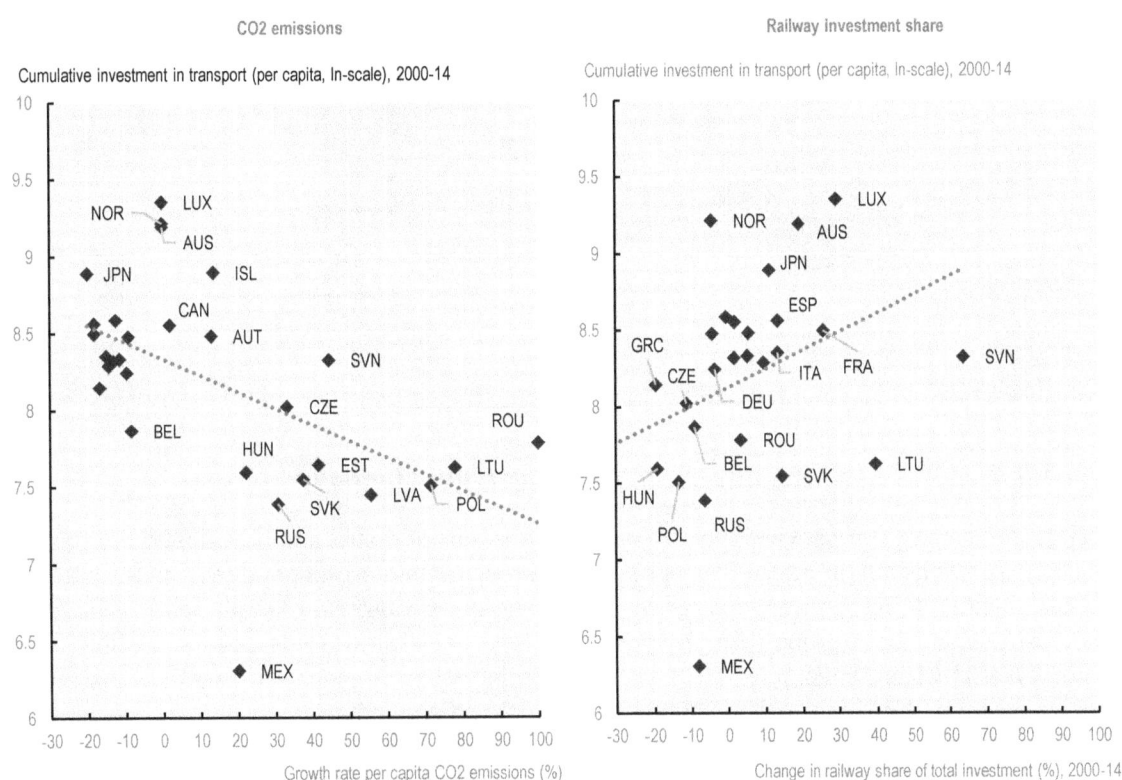

Source: ITF (2019[8]), *ITF Transport Infrastructure Database*, https://doi.org/10.1787/trsprt-data-en (accessed on 29 July 2019).

Households in countries that invested more in infrastructure do not spend more on transport (Figure 1.6). The type of transport expenditure shifts in countries that invested more in infrastructure. Households in those countries tend to spend an increasing share of their transport expenditures on transport services (i.e. not going to the purchase and operation of personal vehicles). This suggests that in countries that invested more in transport infrastructure – and particularly in railway (Figure 1.3) – consumers shifted their spending away from private transport modes and towards transport services, without changing the overall share of spending going to transport.

Figure 1.6. Household expenditures and inland infrastructure investment, 2000-14

Household expenditure on transport

Service share in transport expenditures

Change in transport share of household expenditures
(percentage points), 2000-14

Change in service share in transport expenditures
(percentage points), 2000-14

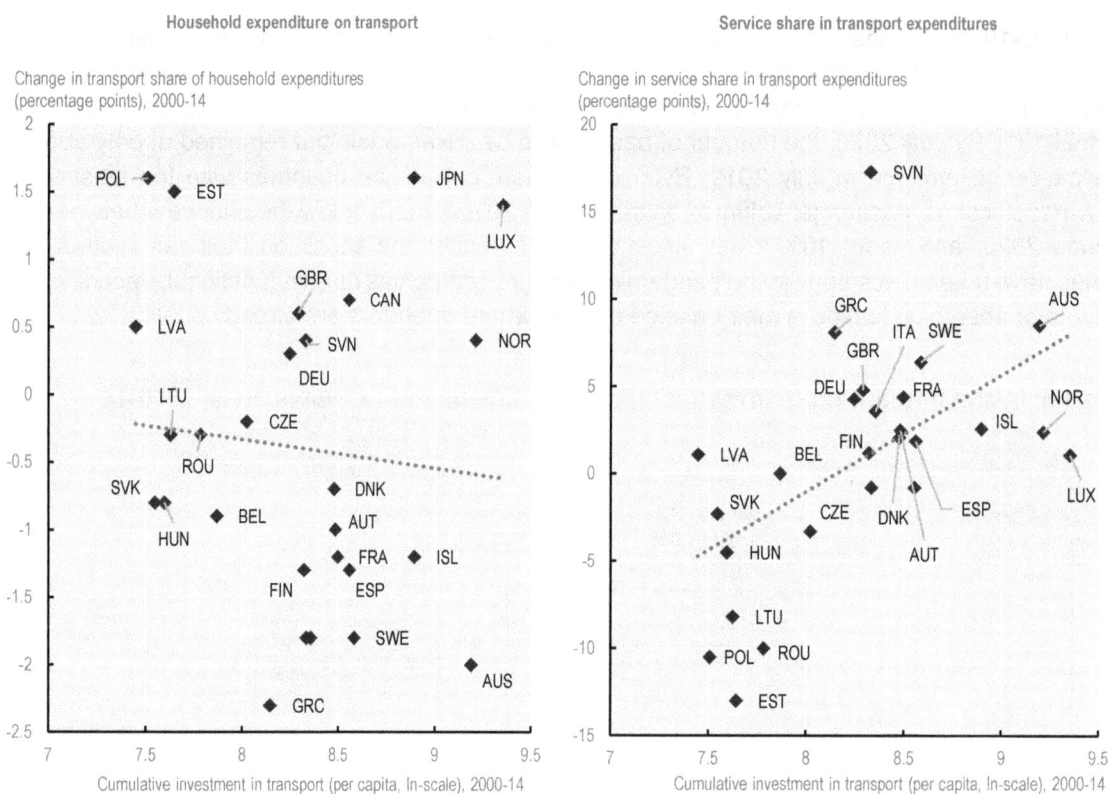

Source: ITF (2019[8]), *ITF Transport Infrastructure Database*, https://doi.org/10.1787/trsprt-data-en (accessed on 29 July 2019).

Investment in metro and high-speed rail has grown substantially

Contrary to the evolution of conventional rail tracks, the length of metro and high-speed rail has grown substantially. Conventional rail tracks (as opposed to metros, trams or high-speed rail) make up 94% of all rail track-kilometres in Europe, North America, China and Japan, but their length has grown very little during 1995-2016 in most regions (IEA, 2019[28]). The most rapid growth has been in the length of the metro networks. In China, India, Japan, Russia, Europe and North America, the length of the metro rail network increased by 4 800 km between 2000 and 2017. China and India have played a determinant role, with 32 out of the 43 cities where a new metro system opened between 2010 and 2017 being located in Asia. The length of the high-speed rail network – the largest share of which is located in China, Japan, Korea and Europe – expanded from approximately 30 000 km to about 70 000 km between 2010 and 2017, with China being responsible for most of the expansion (IEA, 2019[28]). The share of high-speed tracks located in China in 2010 was about 36%. By 2017, this share had risen to 63%. Some countries have seen neither an expansion nor an uptake of the rail network. In Canada and the United States, for instance, the uptake – as measured by the number of passengers per km – was mostly flat between 1995 and 2016, while it nearly doubled worldwide during this period (IEA, 2019[28]).

Rail investment supports the low-carbon transition

Transport investment should shift decisively towards rail, being among the most efficient and lowest-emitting modes of transport when compared to road, maritime and air transport. Rail accounts for only 2% of energy use in the transport sector in spite of carrying 8% of motorised passenger transport and 7% of freight transport (IEA, 2019[28]). The rail share is projected to grow substantially in some of the scenarios elaborated by the International Energy Agency (IEA). For example, in the "high rail scenario", a combination of changes in consumer habits coupled with a shift of transport investment towards rail transport is expected to be matched by an increase in passenger and freight activity by about 6 trillion passenger-kilometres and 3 trillion tonne-kilometres respectively relative to the baseline scenario.[13]

High-speed (HS) rail and urban transport are playing a pivotal role in the changing composition of transport investment needs. HS rail penetration varies widely across countries also because the profitability of this investment hinges on its ability to connect large metropolitan areas. On longer distances, the evidence from existing HS rail lines suggests that around 2 hours' trip time (roughly 3 hours door-to-door), travellers start shifting towards air travel (ITF, 2014[29]). There is less consensus on the necessary population size in the catchment area of HS rail. The profitability of investment depends on a range of demand factors, including price, the connection between metropolitan areas and the wealth of the connected places. Even if there is an expected profitable business case, the high upfront cost of investment can make countries hesitant to shift a large share of their total annual investment into a small number of HS rail lines.

Box 1.2. The Trans-European Transport Network

In Europe, transport infrastructure investment has been a stronghold of EU investment policy since the early 1990s. Since the signing of the Maastricht Treaty in 1993, the Trans-European Transport Network (TEN-T) has been the tool of infrastructure policy in Europe and an important instrument to achieve cohesion and growth of European regions.

Under the current 2014-20 plan, transport infrastructure projects are divided into a core and a comprehensive network based on their priority, with priority projects typically being long-implementation, high-cost and cross-border. The core network is foreseen to be completed by 2030, the second by 2050. The core network is organised into nine main corridors (Figure 1.7) relying on transport via rail, airport and port. Rail transport occupies the centre stage with respect to each of these corridors, with some of the tracts being built *ex novo* and some others being renovated or upgraded. The estimated magnitude of funding required to complete the core network during 2021-30 amounts to EUR 500 billion, a figure that rises to EUR 1.5 trillion if the comprehensive network is also considered (EC, 2017[30]).

Rail investment occupies the largest share of TEN-T funding. In 2015, rails absorbed as much as 51.5% of TEN-T EU-level expenditures, followed by roads (30.6%), ports and motorways (9.2%), airports (5.5%), multimodal infrastructure (2.1%) and inland waterways (1.1%) (EC, 2017[31]). The situation was different in 1997 when roads and rail represented similar shares of TEN-T funding (Puga, 2002[32]). The increase in the share of budget absorbed by rail investment is partly explained by the shift towards high-speed (HS) rail. Despite the aggregate increase in HS rail investment, HS rail penetration was in 2016 still very heterogeneous among the European countries for which data are available (Figure 1.8). Among those European countries, France was the one with the highest share in either dedicated or upgraded railroad, close to 50%, followed by Italy and Spain.

Unlike traditional rail, HS rail – which is typically not suited for the transport of goods – benefits mostly passenger transport. HS rail investments can favour the economic activity of larger cities at the disadvantage of smaller urban centres (Puga, 2002[32]). For instance, multi-establishment firms may find convenient to relocate their headquarters to larger cities where they can benefit from the proximity to the service-producing sector since the reduction in travelling distance makes arm's length relationships no more necessary. The resulting increase in agglomeration in larger cities tends to benefit especially the service-producing sector therein concentrated.

Figure 1.7. The nine major corridors of the 2014-20 TEN-T core network

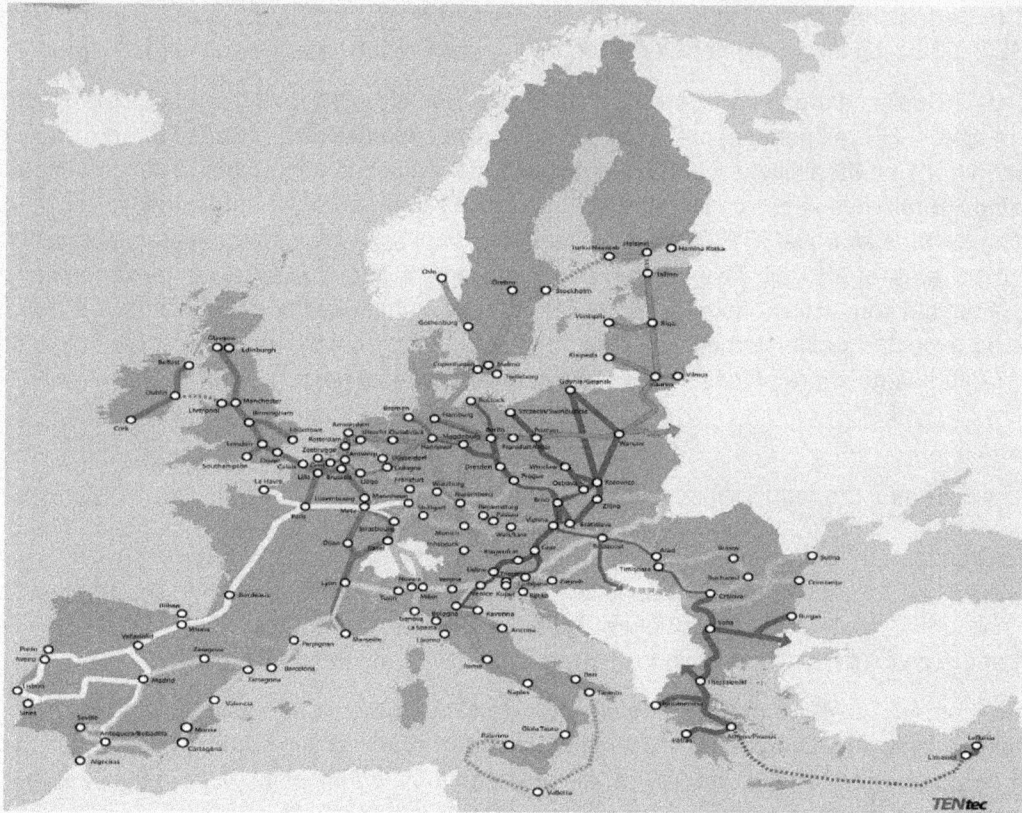

Note: Atlantic corridor (yellow); Baltic-Adriatic (dark blue); Mediterranean (green); North Sea-Baltic (red); North Sea-Mediterranean (violet); Orient- East Med (brown); Rhine-Alpine (orange); Rhine-Danube (light blue); Scandinavian-Mediterranean (pink).
Source: EC (n.d.[33]), *Infrastructure and Investment*, https://ec.europa.eu/transport/themes/infrastructure_en.

Figure 1.8. Composition of the rail network length in selected European countries, 2016

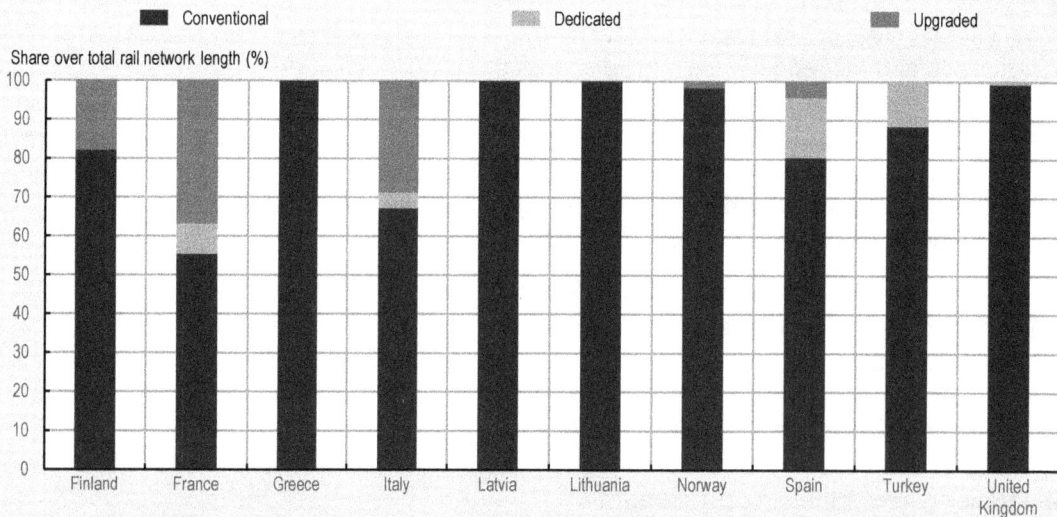

Note: HS rail can be either upgraded from existing rail infrastructure or created as dedicated new lines.
Source: Eurostat (2020[34]), *Railway Transport – Length of Lines, by Maximum Speed (rail_if_line_sp) (database)*.

While the benefits may seem more pronounced for the service sector, the manufacturing sector can also benefit. HS rail indeed reduces the cost of search of suppliers and buyers for individual firms. Hence, firms located in the proximity of HS rail stations can better optimise the size and composition of their network of suppliers and buyers and be more productive (Bernard, Moxnes and Saito, 2019[35]).

Source: EC (2017[30]), *Delivering TEN-T Facts and Figures*, European Commission; EC (2017[31]), *Progress Report on the Implementation of the TEN-T Network in 2014 and 2015*, European Commission; Puga, D. (2002[32]), "Progress report on the implementation of the TEN-T Network in 2014 and 2015", *Journal of Economic Geography*, Vol. 2, pp. 373-406; Bernard, A., A. Moxnes and Y. Saito (2019[35]), *Production Networks, Geography and Firm Performance*.

The still relatively scarce empirical evidence quantifying the benefits of HS rail holds back investment in the expansion of the network.[14] For example, one significant challenge to HS rail network expansion is posed by the fact that, as the network expands, the set of new tracks that is profitable to develop shrinks or, in other words, the expansion of the network does not raise the profitability of other potential tracks sufficiently (ITF, 2014[29]). Traffic volume is an important driver of HS rail investment profitability, which means that, in each country, there exists just a limited set of potentially profitable connecting lines, typically those connecting large urban centres.[15] Moreover, due to the substitutability between air travel and HS rail travel, the distance between endpoints capable of maximising revenues is likely to be between 500 km and 1 000 km, thus further reducing the set of potentially profitable connecting lines (ITF, 2014[29]).

Complementary actions can enhance the profitability of HS rail investment. Urban transport is an important complement to interregional HS rail. Strengthening local public transport systems improves access to HS rail stations. Often, inadequate feeding connections outweigh the timesaving benefits of HS rail (ITF, 2014[29]). For instance, in France, the HS rail network converges on Paris, whose multiple train stations each tend to serve a distinct axis of the network. Hence, without the well-developed metro system in the city centre of Paris, allowing fast travel from one station to another, the gains from the rollout of HS infrastructure in France might have been more modest. The acknowledgement of the complementarity of urban transport to HS rail investment is underscored by the Grand Paris Express project, a 38 billion-worth urban transport investment project in Île-de-France aiming at connecting strategic sites situated in the commuting zone of Paris metropolitan area, ranging from airports and TGV (*Train à grande vitesse*, HS train) stations to employment centres (Institut d'Aménagement et d'Urbanisme, 2013[36]).

Urban transport demands more investment. Despite the share of urban rail in Europe being relatively large (15% compared to 5% in China); further investment is required in European cities to: i) close the gaps in accessibility highlighted in Chapter 2; and ii) adapt urban transport to the needs of a low-carbon transition. Urban transport indeed represents a large share of passenger transport that in turn contributes to 50% of total transport-related emissions (OECD, 2019[37]). Yet, only 35% of the countries that signed the Paris Agreement in 2015 have included public transport in their climate action plans.

Investments favouring the local diffusion of knowledge can increase the return to investments in local connectivity. Investments in the local transport infrastructure help better connect cities with the surrounding rural regions. By reducing the physical distance between workers and firms located in the same region, these investments facilitate the exchange of knowledge and ideas. Local governments can maximise the returns from investments into local transport infrastructure by promoting policies that favour the creation and exchange of ideas. A similar mix of policy interventions was adopted in the West Sweden region that gravitates around the main city of Gothenburg. Regional authorities undertook investments into innovation and research infrastructure, through the creation of, for example, science parks and at the same time strengthened the local transport network, which magnified their returns on both investments (OECD, 2018[38]).

Regional differences in highway investment reflect narrowing infrastructure gaps

In Portugal and Spain but also France and the United Kingdom for example, the highway network has grown considerably between 1990 and 2012. In other countries, the growth has been minimal, either because the highway network was already well developed in 1990 (e.g. Germany or Italy) or because these countries experienced very modest changes in the spatial distribution of economic activity during their period considered. For example, in Scandinavian countries, areas that were little populated in 1990 continued to be so also in 2012, so that the need to build new infrastructure in these countries did not materialise. Finally, in East European countries, such as the Czech Republic Hungary or Poland, there has been little improvement in accessibility for people and firms during the past 20 years and considerable additional effort is needed.

The major expansion of the European highway network shifted from the centre and the south to the east between 1990 and 2012. Since 2000, countries like the Czech Republic started to catch up with the growth rate of the length of the highway network in the region of Severovýchod, located in the north-eastern part of the Czech Republic, was 400% compared to national median growth slightly less than 100%. At the same time, the region of Liguria, Italy, experienced zero growth, as opposed to Umbria, which instead saw the length of the transport network grow by nearly 200%. These very high growth rates can be explained in terms of the nearly absent highway network at the beginning of the sample in the corresponding regions.

Countries where predominantly urban regions grew faster than predominantly rural or intermediate regions expanded their highway network less during 2000-12. Academic studies have established a causal and positive relationship between investment into highways departing from the city centre and the share of people in the suburbs of metropolitan areas.[16] Across OECD countries with available data, there is some evidence that countries with greater expansion of their highway network experienced a greater shift away from predominantly urban areas to predominantly rural or intermediate regions (Figure 1.9). Ireland and Poland in particular stand out.

Figure 1.9. Change in share of people living in predominantly urban regions against growth rate in highways network length

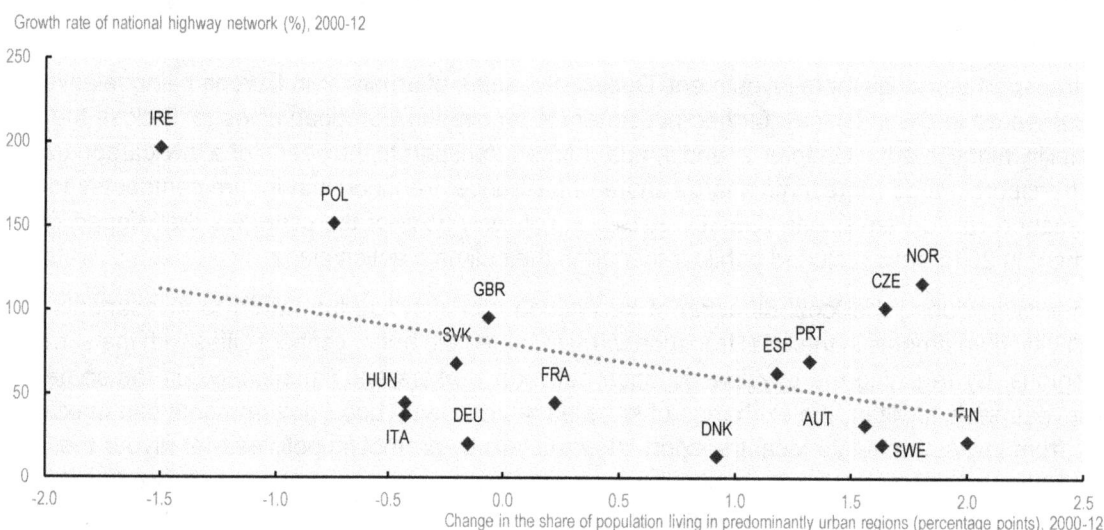

Source: Data on transport network from Stelder, D. (2016[26]), "Regional accessibility trends in Europe: Road infrastructure, 1957-2012", *Regional Studies*, Vol. 50/6, pp. 983-995; data on population from OECD Regional Database.

Box 1.3. Highway expansion in Europe in urban and rural regions

The type of regions with the largest expansion in the highway network between 2000 and 2012, depends on the country (Figure 1.10). In respectively 6 out of 17 countries, the network expanded most in predominantly urban or predominantly rural regions, with the highway network expanding strongest in intermediate regions in the remaining 5 countries. While in East European countries highway investment during this period focused on priority projects, such as endowing the main cities with a highway network, in many Western European countries, such as France or Spain, highway investment aimed at expanding highway penetration in areas where it had been scarce up to that moment, i.e. predominantly rural areas. It follows that in Western European countries, the length of the highway network grew by 52% (41%) in predominantly rural (urban) regions, while the pattern is reversed in East European regions, where highway length grew by 70% (160%) in predominantly rural (urban) regions.

Figure 1.10. Growth of the length of the highway network in TL3 regions, 2000-12

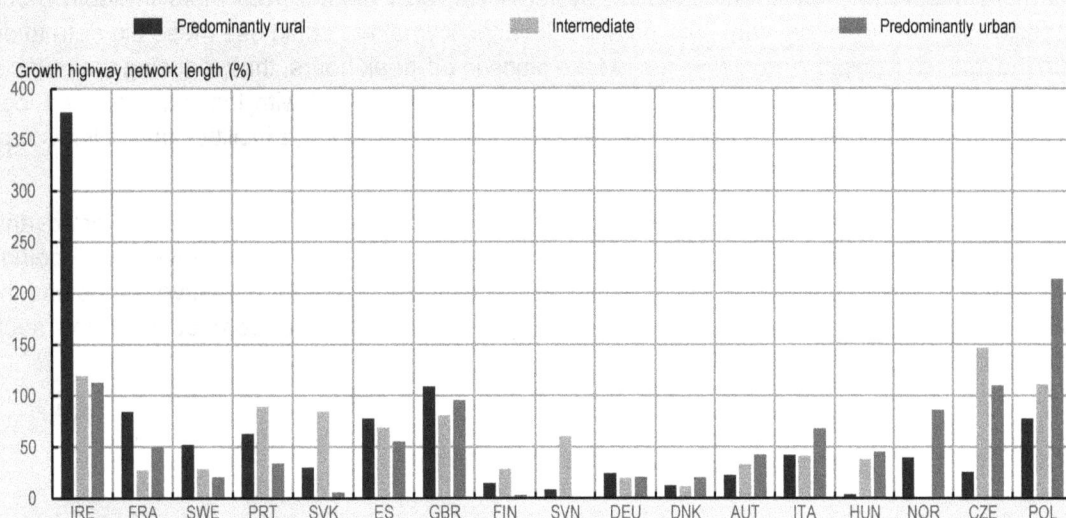

Note: Averages by region type at the TL3 level. Countries are sorted in descending order of the difference between average growth in highway length in predominantly rural and urban regions. The classification of TL3 regions into prevalently rural, intermediate and prevalently urban comes from the OECD Regional Database.
Source: Data on the transport network from Stelder, D. (2016[26]), "Regional accessibility trends in Europe: Road infrastructure, 1957-2012", *Regional Studies*, Vol. 50/6, pp. 983-995.

European regions are not the only ones that witnessed a steep increase in investment in roads. Korea devoted a total budget of KRW 15.8 trillion (USD 14.4 billion) or 1.1% of 2013 GDP road and rail infrastructure investment. The expansion in the road network has been in particular significant, with paved roads in 1951 having a total length of 580 km compared to over 87 000 in 2013, including more than 4 100 km of HS expressways (OECD, 2016[3]).

Maintenance cost account for an increasing share of infrastructure spending

As the expansion of the highway network slows the cost of maintaining existing infrastructure rises. In the United States, for instance, the share of maintenance spending exceeds the one of investment. Real – that is, adjusted for the cost of raw materials – spending on operation and maintenance jumped from USD 243.3 billion to USD 266.5 billion; meanwhile, real spending on capital projects plummeted 16%, from

USD 207.1 billion to USD 174.0 billion between 2007 and 2017 (Brookings Institution, 2019[39]). As the length of the road network expands and as the network matures, the relative importance of maintenance costs relative to new investment will increase. Existing studies document that not only required maintenance costs are large but also that large shortfalls materialise with respect to this expenditure category (McKinsey & Company, 2013[40]), with negative consequences for traffic and road safety.

The highway networks in most developed countries require substantial maintenance spending. Most western countries, built them in the first decades after World War II. As budgets tightened, the state of disrepair of these highway networks has become evident after the Great Recession. Many European countries have been forced to put in place more stringent budget limitations that have contributed to the slack in the recovery of public investments, especially in the European periphery (OECD, 2016[41]).

Maximising the lifespan of roads needs therefore to be a guiding principle of new investments into transport infrastructure (ITF, 2018[42]). From a public finance point of view, it is important to minimise the maintenance cost of each new kilometre added to the existing transport network in order for total maintenance costs not to scale up as rapidly as the rate at which the transport network expands. Big data can be used to forecast growth in transport demand with better accuracy and plan transport infrastructure updates more effectively. Traffic management systems can also benefit from more in-depth modelling made possible by the use of big data. For instance, local policymakers could use these big data to devise a system that makes it possible for deliveries to take place in off-peak hours, thus reducing the traffic strain of roads (ITF, 2018[43]). The establishment of a good co-operation level with the transport and logistics sector can further help local policymakers improve the distribution of storage facilities and collection points on the territory, thus re-equilibrating the traffic strain of certain roads.

The circulation of automated vehicles will likely enhance the efficient use of roads. The major advantages of having automated vehicles circulating on highways will be in terms of safety and drivers' well-being. The slow diffusion that these technologies have had so far is mostly imputable to normative issues and the lag with which regulatory bodies are catching up, from setting the standards for competition in this sector to the rules for data security (ITF, 2018[44]).

Benefits from transport infrastructure investment

Transport infrastructure creates economic benefits through different channels. Importantly, these channels also differ between infrastructures connecting regions and those connecting people within a city. Interregional transport infrastructure facilitates mostly the movement of goods, while within-city transport infrastructure the movement of people. Given that the investments take place at different scales, the competent authorities as well as governance arrangements are different. A companion report on *Improving Transport Planning for Accessible Cities* (OECD, 2020[45]) provides an in-depth discussion of planning and governance arrangements for better outcomes from infrastructure investment. The review of the benefits of transport infrastructure investment provided in the upcoming section deals with each type of infrastructure investment separately.

Evaluating the contribution of different channels is complicated by challenges in measuring the economic benefits of transport infrastructure investment (Box 1.4). The location choice of infrastructure is not random but follows a specific rational (e.g. economic, social, political, etc.). If transport infrastructure is constructed to connect economic hubs with high growth potential in a country (or across countries), any estimate of the economic benefits of the investment risks confounding the contribution of the new infrastructure with the contribution of other factors that led to higher growth potential. Economists have developed a range of strategies to address this challenge that help identify the true "causal" effect of investment.[17] The strategies rely on historic transport networks, geographical characteristics of the area or policy choices that are unrelated to economic considerations, for example, to try to estimate what the economic development in a place would have been in absence of the transport investment. Such a counterfactual approach does come at a price as the question that can be answered "causally" is often not the question that is the most pressing. For example, a road that connects two major metropolitan areas also creates access for less densely populated areas along the way. Finding a causal estimate for the impact of investment on the two major metropolitan areas is very difficult but many studies have developed strategies to identify the impact on the less densely populated areas along its way.

Box 1.4. Challenges in the measurement of infrastructure investment's economic impact

The location of transport infrastructure investment is not random but carefully chosen to optimise economic and social objectives. A comparison of the economic development following the realisation of the new infrastructure between places where investment occurred and others will therefore result in misleading estimates of the realised value for connected places. If investment is, for example, targeted towards areas expected to grow, it is difficult to disentangle how much of the resulting growth can be attributed to the investment itself and how much is due to other factors that promoted growth even before investment took place. What is missing is data on a "counterfactual" state of the world, i.e. what would have been the growth in a region or city where investment took place if that investment had not taken place.

Source: Lee, N. and A. Lembcke (2020[46]), "The economic benefits of accessibility: A survey", Unpublished Manuscript.

Benefits from interregional road and rail infrastructure

While interregional transport infrastructure builds on several transport modes, this section focuses on the benefits associated with road (and in particular highways) and rail infrastructure investment. These 2 modes together accounted in 2015 for 93% of worldwide surface freight transport (ITF, 2019[27]) and 73% of worldwide non-urban passenger transport (ITF, 2017[47]).

Highways and railways have a long history in most OECD countries. Railways construction started during the second half of the 19th century in many countries (e.g. Europe, Australia, Canada, Japan, United States, etc.). For example, in 1840, total length in kilometres of European rail was close to zero. In 1910, it was greater than 200 000 km, more than what it was in 2010 (Martí-Henneberg, 2013[48]). The first modern highways were built from the 1940s onwards driven by the advent of mass production of automobiles and the highway network continues to expand today. The upcoming section draws lessons from a recent set of studies assessing the economic benefits associated with transport infrastructure investments in OECD member countries.[18] The results highlight that interregional transport infrastructure investment is likely to benefit some regions but can create adverse economic effects in regions with worse access to infrastructures or, in some cases, in regions where access improves. Careful evaluation is required to ensure that infrastructures provide a positive aggregate net impact.

Interregional transport infrastructure allows for deeper trade integration

Transport infrastructure reduces the cost of shipping goods from one region to another. The costs associated with the shipment of goods typically fall under the umbrella of trade costs, which includes two broad types of costs. The first type of costs is those that arise due to the physical distance between trading partners. These generalised transport costs include both non-pecuniary costs, such as the opportunity cost of travel time required to ship goods, and pecuniary costs, such as fuel costs, taxes and fees, and other operating costs (Combes and Lafourcade, 2005[49]). The second type is costs stemming from the countries' trading partners reciprocal trade policies (e.g. tariffs). As infrastructure investment tends to be an important tool for regional development, it is necessary to consider the wider range of policies and regulatory barriers that facilitate or hinder trade, in particular for major infrastructure that connects across country borders.[19]

Better transport infrastructure reduces the cost of shipping goods and magnifies the impact of other cost-reducing measures. For example, in France, the development of the highway network between 1978 and 1998 led to a 3.2% reduction in transport costs. Compared against a generalised reduction of 38% percentage points, transport infrastructure accounts, therefore, for one-tenth of the overall cost reduction. Other measures had a larger impact, the decline in fuel price and fuel consumption accounted for a 6% reduction in transport costs and lower labour costs (partly due to higher productivity and partly due to lower per capita wages) for a further 5.5%. While improvements in the transport network did not contribute as much in absolute terms to the overall decline, they shaped the geography of the gains resulting from other cost-reducing measures. Areas with better transport infrastructure had stronger economic gains than those with worse infrastructure (Combes and Lafourcade, 2005[49]).[20]

Lower transport costs reduce prices for intermediates and consumer goods produced by firms located farther away. Consumers gain unequivocally through lower average prices and access to a wider variety of goods that they can purchase. For the United States, for example, an estimate suggests that the value of the expanded variety of imported goods between 1972 and 2001 amounted to 2.6% of GDP for US consumers (Broda and Weinstein, 2006[50]). Firms also gain better access to intermediate inputs produced by firms located farther away and sold at a lower price. Some firms, however, do not benefit from better infrastructure connection. Firms that produce with less cost efficiency are at a higher risk of being outcompeted by more distant and competitive firms, in particular when they produce highly standardised products. Conversely, firms that produce more complex or tailored inputs, as well as those that produce more cost efficiently have the opportunity to seize a larger market share. An example is a change in domestic supply links in Japan after the Chinese accession to the World Trade Organization (WTO). Estimates based on 4.5 million buyer-seller links show that local production networks were strengthened (in particular for non-standardised inputs) and that offshoring and sourcing from outside the country reduced the attractiveness of domestic suppliers that produce standardised inputs and that are located further away from the sourcing firm (Furusawa et al., 2017[51]).

Benefits of new transport infrastructure depend on the accessibility it provides

The gains for a given region depend on how many new customers can be reached via the improved transport network. Simply building a highway is not sufficient for economic growth to materialise in a given region. The crucial question is what improvements in accessibility the new infrastructure provides. The average income level – proxying for expenditure capacity – of the new markets accessible by the region is one way to capture accessibility (see Box 1.5). Accessibility and overall gains also depend on the wider transport network. If the additional infrastructure connects to an existing network with good accessibility or improves access to existing logistic centres, ports or airports, it is more likely to support significant benefits in terms of freight traffic volumes. The Megaregion of Western Scandinavia – covering the regions along the western coast from Oslo via Gothenburg to Malmö and Øresund – is a major freight hub for Norway and Sweden. It hosts Norway's largest airport, Sweden's two largest ports and connecting road infrastructure that has been improved in recent years. In contrast, there is a lack of fast rail infrastructure crossing from Norway into Sweden and between the second- and third-largest cities in Sweden. Trains have gradually lost competitiveness to roads, particularly on the Oslo-Gothenburg route (OECD, 2018[38]).

Additional highways tend to create better market access but gains vary across regions. Roads are essentially a means to fulfil a certain need, such as the exchange of goods between two places but the construction of a road in itself does not necessarily generate such need, therefore potentially failing to create a market where it does not exist. In support of this argument, the correlation between the evolution of market access and the evolution of highway length across TL3 regions during 2000-12 is far from perfect (Figure 1.11). In about 40% of the 743 TL3 regions for which data are available, the growth rate in market access between 2000 and 2012 was lower than the one expected given the growth rate in highway length during the same period.[21] In Spain, for example, between 1980 and 2000, market access improved in almost all municipalities because of the highway network construction but the improvements were more pronounced in the most peripheral regions (Holl, 2007[52]). Due to the non-automatic relation between road length and market access, the use of changes in road length as a proxy for the opportunities unlocked by transport infrastructure investment can be quite misleading and metrics based on market access should be preferred.

Figure 1.11. Growth rate of market access and highway length in European TL3 regions, 2000-12

Growth rate GDP market access 2000-12 for TL3 regions (%)

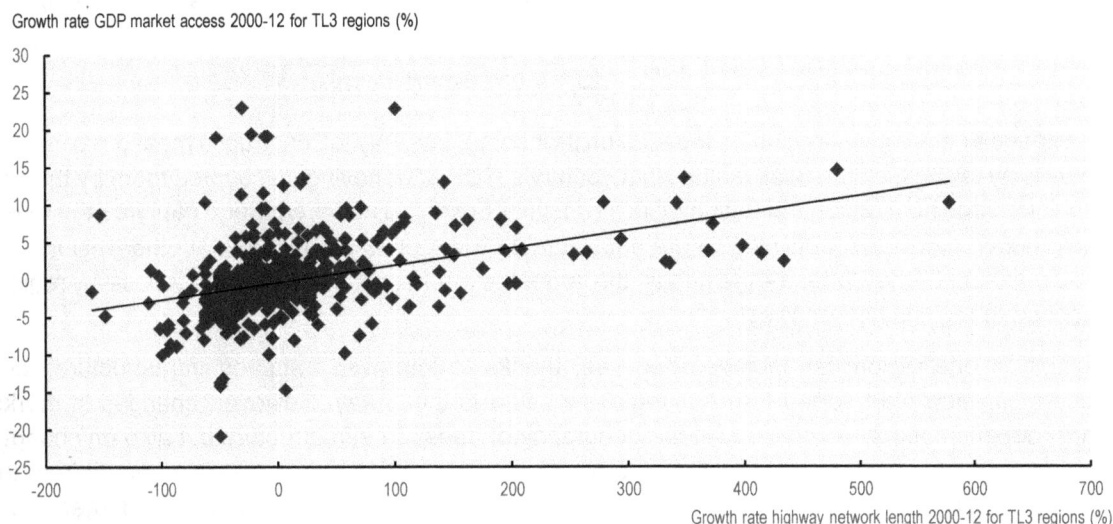

Growth rate highway network length 2000-12 for TL3 regions (%)

Note: Both variables have been demeaned with respect to the sample average. A total of 743 TL3 regions are considered. All original EU member states (Belgium, France, Germany, Italy, Luxembourg, the Netherlands and the United Kingdom), Greece, which joined the EU in 1981, the 1986 EU additions (Portugal and Spain) and one 1995 EU addition (Austria) and all other Southern and East European countries that joined the EU later are included.
Source: Data based on from Stelder, D. (2016[26]), "Regional accessibility trends in Europe: Road infrastructure, 1957-2012", *Regional Studies*, Vol. 50/6, pp. 983-995; Adler, M. et al. (2020[53]), "Roads, market access and regional economic development", OECD Regional Development Working Papers, OECD Publishing, Paris.

Accessibility increases by building new infrastructure and through growth in already connected regions. An important feature of infrastructure is that once a road is in place, continuous economic improvements in one place along its path can create positive spill-overs to other connected places. Transport connections can therefore create lasting stimulus by benefitting from the success of connected places. In a study for 28 European countries, road infrastructure construction is the main determinant for accessibility improvements when fewer mobile factors are considered. For accessibility to population, 66% of the increase in accessibility between 1990 and 2012 comes from improved road infrastructure. In contrast, for more mobile factors (such as employment and GDP), growth in connected areas becomes more important. For GDP, only 18% of the accessibility improvements can be attributed to new or better roads, the remaining 82% stem from economic growth in already connected places and in case of access to employment the two aspects are roughly equally important (Adler et al., 2020[53]).

Box 1.5. An accessibility-based measure of potential economic gains

The notion of "market access" – how the term "accessibility" is translated by trade economists – is central to the field of New Economic Geography (NEG). At the core of NEG models is a rigorous treatment of the various determinants of the location decision of workers and firms. When there are transport costs, the decision on where to locate depends both on the size of the market reachable given the available transport network and on the unit cost of production.

The potential economic gains from transport infrastructure investment for a region are proportional to changes in market potential, where one way to measure market potential is (Adler et al., 2020[53]):

$$Market\ Potential_r = \sum_{m \in M} \frac{Gross\ Domestic\ Product_m}{Transport\ Cost_{r,m}^d}$$

Since expenditure in a given region m depends on its income, one way to construct a measure of market potential is by taking the sum of all regions in a country's GDP after having discounted them by the cost of shipping goods from region r to region m, or $Transport\ Cost_{r,m}^d$. The parameter d captures the extent to which goods produced in one region are substitutable with goods produced in another region. The more substitutable – the higher d – the goods, the larger the market potential offered by close-by regions as opposed to regions further away.

Production in one region can increase because, thanks to improved transport infrastructure, local producers can now start selling to richer regions located farther away. However, changes in market potential depend not only on changes in the geography of transport infrastructure but also on changes in the geography of economic activity. Firms located in a small region can in principle benefit from the construction of a new highway connecting to a larger one. However, if firms located in the larger region are more competitive in a larger share of industries, consumers located in the small region will want to purchase their products. A labour supply shortage in the larger region will drive local wages up, and eventually be filled either via commuting or via actual immigration from the nearby small region. In either case, market potential will dry up in the small region, thereby reinforcing the relocation of firms towards the larger one.

The economic development of cities in the People's Republic of China following the construction of the highway network starting in 1988 exemplifies the potential trade-offs inherent in infrastructure development. The network was conceived with the idea of promoting economic activity in hinterland prefectures but had the opposite result. "Primate" cities – the largest prefectures located within one day's drive from hinterland prefectures – specialised in manufacturing for which they enjoyed a comparative advantage. Manufacturing created jobs that produced more value-added and therefore paid higher wages, which attracted workers to primate cities. They grew in employment and population at the expense of nearby hinterland prefectures that shrank in size and specialise in agriculture (Baum-Snow et al., 2016[17]).

Source: Adler, M. et al. (2020[53]), "Roads, market access and regional economic development", OECD Regional Development Working Papers, OECD Publishing, Paris; Baum-Snow, N. et al. (2016[17]), "Highways, market access, and urban growth in China".

Market access improvements promote regional economic development. Adler et al. (2020[53]) estimate the impact of accessibility improvements that the expansion of the road network and the growth of Europe created between 1990 and 2012 on GDP, employment and population. A 10% increase in market access (in terms of GDP) in other regions increases the GDP in a region by 2% on average. To put this into perspective, Haute-Garonne, the French *département* where Toulouse, France's fifth-largest metropolitan area, is located, benefitted from a significant improvement in the highway network in the southwest of

France and in Spain. The result was an increase in accessibility in terms of GDP of nearly 40% between 1990 and 2012 with about 60% of that improvement during the first 10 years of the period. Madrid, Spain's capital city, became the centre of the country's rapidly expanding highway network during the period but the more peripheral location within Europe meant that the accessibility gains were smaller than in Toulouse, about 30% in terms of GDP accessibility, with half of the gains already realised between 1990 and 2000. But even this smaller improvement translates to 6% additional GDP over the 22-year period due to improvements in accessibility. For other outcomes, the impact is even stronger than for GDP. Employment in regions, where accessibility to employment outside the region improved by 10%, grew on average by 7%. For the population, the impact is of 6% in a similar order of magnitude. Combined, these results show that better accessibility helps regions grow but also that new opportunities support mainly activities that are in lower value-added and lower productivity sectors, as GDP grows less than employment or population.

The benefits of new infrastructure depend on the existing network with the strongest gains in places closing infrastructure gaps (Adler et al., 2020[53]). Estimates for regions in Eastern Europe for the 1990-2012 period show benefits from market access improvements in terms of GDP and per capita GDP. This is in line with an expansion of economic activity that was stronger for sectors with high value-added, capturing the expansion of manufacturing activities and the integration of regions in new EU member countries in European (or global) value chains. In contrast, market access increased employment in Southern European regions but these did not translate into GDP gains, i.e. employment improvements appear to have mainly fostered growth in low- and medium-income jobs as GDP gains and per capita GDP gains are statistically insignificant. The benefits from improved accessibility arise mainly through the integration with the European-wide road network. When estimates are limited to access improvements within three hours of driving, roughly equivalent to the distance of a business daytrip, the results remain positive but are reduced in magnitude by a factor of four. The market access benefits from European integration and trade are substantially larger than those at the regional level and those for smaller clusters of regions.

Trade and productivity along highways

Improvements in road accessibility create trade-driven growth opportunities for both existing firms and new entrepreneurs. These opportunities materialise either via direct links with the new markets or via indirect links operating through supply chains. Most studies analysing the economic impact of highway construction find evidence of a rise in the total number of active firms in the regions benefitting from highway investment. For example, following the dramatic improvements in the British road network between 1960 and 1990, a 10% increase in accessibility in a neighbourhood (electoral ward with an average population of 6 000 inhabitants) led to a 3%-4% increase in the number of firms (Gibbons et al., 2019[54]). A few studies are also able to differentiate whether the rise in the number of firms is driven by fewer firm deaths or more firm births, finding evidence of an increase in the birth rate of firms (Holl, 2004[55]; 2004[56]). These studies recognise that new firms can be displaced from other regions. In Spain, following the construction of the motorway network, the birth rate of firms in municipalities between 10 km and 20 km away from the new motorways dropped by 13.5 percentage points between 1980 and 1994 relative to the birth rate in municipalities within 10 km from the new motorways (Holl, 2004[55]).

Opportunities for trade increase labour demand. Employment increases both at the aggregate and the plant levels in the regions receiving a highway connection. For example, following the dramatic improvements in the British road network between 1960 and 1990, a 10% increase in accessibility led to a 3%-4% increase in local employment (Gibbons et al., 2019[54]).[22] Moreover, the effects are larger for large and manufacturing-oriented firms, i.e. those that are more likely to trade over longer distances within the country or export their goods (Audretsch, Dohse and Pereira dos Santos, 2017[57]).

Wages can go up in regions receiving a highway connection (Sanchis-Guarner, 2012[58]; Gibbons et al., 2019[54]; Chandra and Thompson, 2000[59]). For example, following the expansion of the British road network between 1960 and 1990, a 10% increase in accessibility results in an increase in average wages of around 2.5%-3% (Gibbons et al., 2019[54]). The increase in wages can be a consequence of rising labour shortages, i.e. the increase in labour demand outpaces the supply of labour. However, continued increases in wages are unlikely to be driven by labour shortages. In the case of longer term increases in wages the likely channel is an increase in productivity in local firms. For example, Gibbons et al. (2019[54]) find the firm-level productivity increase following the improvement in accessibility in the UK to be of the same order of magnitude as the increase in average wages. In India, following the construction of the Golden Quadrilateral, manufacturing productivity growth during 2000-09 in districts located less than 10 km away from the new highways was 2 percentage points higher than in districts located more than 50 km away from the new highways (Ghani, Goswami and Kerr, 2016[60]). Moreover, aggregate productivity can also increase thanks to a more efficient allocation of resources, i.e. workers taking jobs in firms that are more productive and investment flowing into those firms. This is what happened for example in India following the construction of the Golden Quadrilateral: industries with a larger share of employment located close to the new highways gained more in terms of allocative efficiency, i.e. in terms of the likelihood of more productive plants being also of larger size (Ghani, Goswami and Kerr, 2016[60]).

More efficient transport infrastructure can facilitate the spread of ideas and boost local innovation. Agrawal, Galasso and Oettl (Agrawal, Galasso and Oettl, 2017[61]) find that in the United States a 10% increase in the stock of highways in 1983 at the metropolitan level translated into 1.7% more regional patenting during 1983-88. While patents are only an imperfect measure of innovation, it is reasonable to believe that competition among firms increases after an increase in connectedness. Hence, to the extent that product market competition is a solid driver of innovative activity (Aghion and Akcigit, 2015[62]), a reduction in transport costs should also be expected to lead to an increase in innovative activity.

Trade and productivity along railways

Historically, access to the railway network is an important driver of long-term growth. Studies on the economic impact of railway expansion tend to consider population growth as their outcome of interest.[23] The unequivocal finding from studies focusing on the early years of the railway expansion is that access puts cities on a path of steadily higher population growth compared to other cities (Hornung, 2015[63]; Atack et al., 2010[64]; Berger and Enflo, 2015[65]; Büchel and Kyburz, 2016[66]; Donaldson and Hornbeck, 2015[67]). For example, Hornung (2015[63]) finds that the population grew in cities that benefitted from railway access 2.1 percentage points more compared to cities that did not during 1849–71. As these studies focus on cities in the late 19th century, they show the importance of initial connections while the transport network expanded. The effect comes from the reduction in transport cost that raises the value of production and land (in these historic studies primarily the value of agricultural land). The strength of effects today is likely weaker as highways, trucks and cars provide suitable substitutes for many trips.

High-speed (HS) rail investment provides economic benefits if major economic hubs anchor the routes. Ahlfeldt and Feddersen (2018[68]) find that 10 percentage point faster growth in market access following the construction of a HS railway between Cologne and Frankfurt leads to 2-3 percentage point higher GDP per growth during 1992-2006. Similar results are found by Carbo et al. (2019[69]) for the HS rail corridor connecting Madrid to Barcelona. The main difference between traditional and HS railway investment is that while traditional railway also serves the purpose of shipping goods, HS railway eases passenger traffic and business trips. Therefore, while the first-order impact of traditional railway investment is likely to be on the manufacturing sector, the most likely consequences of HS railway investment are trade in services and a reorganisation of production in multi-establishment firms. A cautionary note is that the cost of HS railway investment is high, both for the initial development and for the subsequent operation of the lines. Most currently existing lines connect major cities with substantial passenger flows between them. The costs and required subsidies vary substantially even between these major lines (Albalate and Bel, 2012[70]), which means that any development requires careful evaluation of the potential demand.

The effect of shutting down a railway is negative. Most academic studies focus on the development of new infrastructure, few studies analyse the impact of disinvestments, partly due to the rarity in the occurrence of disinvestment projects. The economic interest for this type of projects should be high given that current infrastructure faces the risk of becoming obsolete in face of newer technologies. Gibbons, Heblich and Pinchbeck (2019[71]) find that the national railway disinvestment of unprofitable lines that took place in the United Kingdom during the 1950s through the 1970s contributed to the decline in rural population. For local communities, a 10% decrease in accessibility due to the dismantlement of the railway network between 1951 and 1981 is associated with a population 3 percentage points lower in 1981 than in a district where market access did not change. The population shifted towards cities and rural areas in the North West and Central England because of the rail cuts in areas of Scotland, South West England and Wales. The major benefactors were the largest UK cities. Without the disinvestment, London and its commuting area would have had 9% less population in 2001. Other major cities such as Birmingham, Glasgow and Manchester would also have had a lower population.

The limitations of transport infrastructure benefits

The potential gains from infrastructure improvements are finite. A counterfactual exercise for EU countries considers providing "perfect" accessibility in all regions by upgrading the existing secondary road network to highways (the roads with the fastest speeds). The results of Adler et al. (2020[53]) suggest that predicted gains in terms of GDP are, on average, between 17% and 26%, with highest remaining gains for regions in Eastern Europe. Predictions for employment and population gains are slightly larger. Overall, the already well-develop highway network provides a high degree of accessibility in many parts of continental Europe but there are still places remaining where benefits can be substantial, especially in Eastern Europe. Additional interventions should, of course, follow best practices and be subject to careful CBA in line with best practices in OECD member countries.

The gains in one region can come at the expense of another region. An example is the response by firms to the construction of the Portuguese motorway system between 1986 and 1997. New firms chose to locate in municipalities located in a 10-kilometre corridor from new motorways, at the expense of the municipalities located outside the corridors (Holl, 2004[55]). In the United States, earnings in counties that became connected to the Interstate Highway System between 1969 and 1993 rose whereas earnings declined in those without access (Chandra and Thompson, 2000[59]) relative to the evolution of the average wage in each state and year. The concentration of economic activity comes also at a cost as agglomeration benefits are balanced by agglomeration costs (Box 1.6).

Aggregate gains depend on whether a new economic activity is created and on the extent to which workers and firms relocate to take advantage of new opportunities. Aggregate gains are maximised when new infrastructure gives rise to new economic activity (gains from *additionality*) possibly in a country's more productive regions (gains from *improved allocative efficiency*) without subtracting resources from the other regions (losses from *displacement*). The demand for new hires and investments generated in a region by new infrastructure is met by tapping into both local resources and those initially located in other regions. Since there are no restrictions to the mobility of workers, local job seekers as well as job seekers living in other regions and willing to relocate may try to take advantage of the new employment opportunities associated with the demand for new economic activity. Combes, Gobillon and Lafourcade (2019[72]) show that the aggregate gains for France from the Grand Paris Express project would be maximised if the new jobs created by the project were filled by individuals that never lived in France, as opposed to individuals moving from other regions of France to Paris.[24] Indeed, in the most common case in which the demand for new economic activity in the region receiving the new infrastructure is also met by tapping into resources initially located in other regions, the aggregate gains will be given by the gains for this region *minus* the losses in terms of economic activity experienced by other regions.

Benefits from infrastructure investment are clearly outweighed by indirect costs in two extreme cases. The first is when the new infrastructure merely triggers a redistribution of economic activity across initially similar regions. In this case, one region merely gains resources (e.g. workers) at the expenses of another region with similar characteristics. The second is when capital investment that follows infrastructure investment would have taken place in any case absent of infrastructure. In both cases, gains from additionality and gains from improved allocative efficiency fail to materialise.

Aside from these two extreme cases, the aggregate effect tends to be positive. Whether benefits outweigh adverse effects depends on the balance between the gains from additionality and the gains (losses) from improved (worsened) allocative efficiency. For instance, the new infrastructure can trigger in the recipient region other forms of capital investment that would have taken place however in other parts of the country absent of the infrastructure. Gains from additionality fail to materialise in this case as well. However, the project can still have an aggregate net positive value if it redistributes resources towards more productive regions. New infrastructure can trigger in the recipient region other forms of capital investment that would not have taken place in any other parts of the country absent of the infrastructure. In this case, the project presents gains from additionality. Nevertheless, the aggregate net positive value is reduced if resources are pulled away from more productive regions in order to satisfy the new demand for labour created by the infrastructure. These potential losses from worsened allocative efficiency can be averted if the project succeeds in attracting unutilised local resources into production, for instance by tapping into a situation of high unemployment or low labour force participation (Venables, Laird and Overman, 2014[73]).

Agglomeration shadows can outweigh the benefits of better access. In a seminal study, Vickerman, Spiekermann and Wegener (1999[74]) argue that the promotion of HS transport networks across Europe would benefit already well-connected core areas over peripheral areas that the investment in transport connection aims to support. Better connections may help smaller cities benefit from agglomeration economies in large cities but may also lead to agglomeration shadows where firms in the core start serving the market in the surrounding area at the expense of local businesses. Transport infrastructure investment may therefore amplify differences among *ex ante* asymmetric regions.

One of the reasons for which pre-existing gaps may be amplified is the existence of agglomeration economies, i.e. productivity advantages from co-location (Box 1.6). As accessibility in a region improves, firms can serve a wider market. The larger market potential attracts new firms thanks to economies of scale, i.e. the fact that the firm's average cost declines as output increases. In choosing where to locate, firms can also reap the benefits from locating in already dense areas, next to already existing firms and close to a larger pool of workers, i.e. they can also reap "agglomeration benefits". The productivity gains from co-location mean that firms are more productive, which allows them to pay better wages and thereby attract more workers, and in turn attract more firms. Estimates for Chinese rural prefectures following the construction of the highway network started in 1988 show that this is the case as "primate cities" connected by new highways drew in workers from nearby rural prefectures. The rural prefectures lost population and manufacturing employment following the construction of the highway network (Baum-Snow et al., 2016[17]).

Inequality within regions can increase in response to infrastructure investment. Efforts to improve accessibility may also differentially affect different groups, with skilled workers often benefitting at the expense of the less well qualified (Fretz, Parchet and Robert-Nicoud, 2017[75]). Michaels (2008[76]) finds that labour demand for skilled workers increased during 1959-75 more in counties traversed by the US interstate highway system compared to the rest. Fretz et al. (2017[75]) find that the share of top taxpayers increased by 24% between 1947 and 2010 in areas located within 10 km of access to the new highway network in Switzerland. They argue that this is because high-income workers can benefit more than proportionately from the opportunities offered by tighter trade integration.

Box 1.6. Agglomeration economies: Benefits and costs

Metropolitan areas and dynamic medium-sized cities have enormous potential for job creation and innovation as they are hubs and gateways for global networks such as trade or transport. In many OECD member countries, labour productivity (measured in terms of GDP per worker) and wages can be observed to increase with city size.

Stronger productivity levels are a reflection of a bonus intrinsic to being in a city, known as the agglomeration benefit. On average, a worker's wage increases with the size of the city where he/she works, even after controlling for worker attributes such as education level. OECD estimates suggest that agglomerations benefit in the form of a wage premium rises by 2%-5% for a doubling of population size (Ahrend et al., 2014[77]), which is in line with comparable studies for individual countries (Combes et al., 2012[78]). However, agglomeration benefits do not accrue homogeneously across cities and they show sizeable variations within countries.

Higher productivity is due in part to the quality of the workforce and the industrial mix. Larger cities on average have a more educated population, with the shares of both very high-skilled and low-skilled workers increasing with city size. A 10 percentage point increase in the share of university-educated workers in a city raises the productivity of other workers in that city by 3%-4% (Ahrend et al., 2014[77]). Larger cities typically have a higher proportion of sectors with higher productivity, such as consulting, legal or financial services, etc. They are also more likely to be hubs or service centres through which trade flows and financial and other flows are channelled. These flows typically require the provision of high value-added services.

Living in large cities does provide benefits but it also has disadvantages. While productivity, wages and the availability of many amenities generally increase with city size, so do what is generally referred to as agglomeration costs. Some agglomeration costs are financial: for example, housing prices/rents and, more generally, price levels are typically higher in larger cities. In addition, a number of non-pecuniary costs, such as pollution, congestion, inequality and crime, typically also increase with city size, while trust and similar measures of social capital often decline. Survey data from European cities confirm that citizens in larger cities – despite valuing the increased amenities – are generally less satisfied with the other aspects mentioned, notably air pollution.

To some extent, city size is the outcome of a trade-off between these benefits and costs. Mobility across and within cities implies that – at least in the medium to long term – wage levels, commuting costs and other urban (dis)amenities are reflected in land prices, and more generally in a city's cost of living. This is supported by findings suggesting that for increasing population size, these agglomeration benefits and costs go up at a broadly comparable pace (see Combes et al. (2012[78]) for evidence on France and Gibbons et al. (2011[79]) for the United Kingdom). A similar picture emerges when looking directly at cities' productivity and price levels. Evidence from Germany shows that, on average, increases in a city's productivity, and hence wages, are matched by similar increases in local price levels.

Source: OECD (2015[80]), *OECD Urban Policy Reviews: Mexico 2015: Transforming Urban Policy and Housing Finance*, https://doi.org/10.1787/9789264227293-en.

Benefits from urban transport infrastructure

Economic benefits

Improvements of the public transport network in cities raise firm productivity and the value of land and housing around the stops. Firm productivity responds to the densification around stops and the associated economies of agglomeration (Box 1.6). House prices in the areas affected by the construction or refurbishment of the public transport network tend to rise in response. As areas become more accessible, residents can gain better access to opportunities, whether services or jobs, and therefore housing demand in these areas increases.

An increase in house prices signals that a given transport infrastructure investment succeeded in the goal of improving accessibility and welfare. Gibbons and Machin (2004[81]) evaluate the impact on house prices of the construction of new stations under improvements made to the London Underground and Docklands Light Railway in South East London in the late 1990s. They find that house prices in the areas affected by the transport investment increased by 9.3 percentage points more than the other areas during 1997-2001. Based on the same transport innovation, Pogonyi et al. (2019[82]) find that areas located in the proximity of the new metro line saw their productivity and the total number of plants increase, while areas located farther away saw the total number of plants decrease but no change in productivity. Billings (2011[83]) estimates that light rail transit in Charlotte, North Carolina, led to an increase in the price of single-family properties of 4% and 11.3% for condominiums sold within 1 mile of light rail transit stations. Ahlfeldt et al. (2015[84]) find that city blocks located in the proximity of the Berlin wall and farther away from 1936 subway stations experienced a smaller loss in the price of floor space as a consequence of the city division. Finally, Mayer and Trevien (2017[85]) find that places that received an RER connection in Paris witnessed higher employment growth between 1970 and 1990 but also experienced higher rates of gentrification. Evidence that considers the benefits of Seoul's bus rapid transit system finally also finds strong positive effects on densification and land prices around the system's stops (Cervero and Kang, 2011[86]), with land price premiums of up to 10% estimated for residences within 300 m of bus rapid transit stops.

Broader socio-economic benefits

Transport infrastructure investment matters also for a broader range of socio-economic outcomes at the neighbourhood level. For instance, the expansion of light rail in 16 major US cities during 1970-2000 had very heterogeneous impacts on segregation patterns. "Walk and Ride" stations attracted skilled residents, while "Park and Ride" suburban stations often experienced an increase in poverty (Kahn, 2007[87]). Moreover, the improvement of public transport, especially in city centres, coincided with a trend of increasing concentration of poor households in central cities, while skilled residents who are less public transport-dependent could migrate to suburban areas (Glaeser, Kahn and Rappaport, 2008[88]). Based on data on the full Facebook social network in the United States, Bailey et al. (2019[89]) find that the shape of the transport network is a more effective predictor of social connectedness between any two places than the mere physical distance. These findings stress the importance of the transport policy when it comes to achieving certain policy objectives such as social inclusiveness.

Studies analysing the impact of transport infrastructure investment in cities would benefit from the adoption of an accessibility-based measure. Currently, most studies use the density of the transport network as a proxy for the exposure to potential gains from transport infrastructure investment. This choice is motivated partly by the lack of detailed data on the distribution of economic activity within cities. However, this is also a potentially important oversight since, as already discussed, transport infrastructure investment is not important per se but rather because of its role at connecting people to jobs, producers to consumers, etc. Accessibility measures help capture this aspect (see Chapter 2 for more on accessibility measures).

Effects of transport infrastructure on the reorganisation of economic activity

Urban highways lead to suburbanisation in metropolitan areas and job growth. Radial segments of the highway network departing from the city centre cause a move of people into the suburbs.[25] Looking at different types of transport infrastructure, Baum-Snow et al. (2017[90]) find that radial highways displaced 4% of the central city population in Chinese cities to surrounding regions and ring roads displaced about an additional 20%. Duranton and Turner (2012[91]) assess the overall impact of broadly defined road density on city growth between 1983 and 2003 and find that a 10% increase in the stock of highway causes a 1.5% rise in local employment in US cities. This finding is confirmed in some OECD member countries. Brandily and Rauch (2018[92]) show that Sub-Saharan cities that experienced a weaker increase in road density in the city centre also saw a population growing at a lower rate.

Transport infrastructure investment not only causes suburbanisation in cities but also triggers a reorganisation of economic activity in metropolitan areas. For example, transport infrastructure investment in China displaced economic activity away from central cities towards the suburbs, not just population, and that more specifically, each radial railroad reduced central city industrial GDP by about 20%, with ring roads displacing an additional 50% (Baum-Snow et al., 2017[90]). Garcia-López, Hémet and Viladecans-Marsal (Garcia-López, Hémet and Viladecans-Marsal, 2017[93]) show that the construction of rail station in Paris between 1968 and 2010 reinforced the polycentric nature of the city, leading to the emergence of several sub-centres in the proximity of the new railway stations. These effects are however not universal.

The reorganisation of economic activity depends on the sectors. Baum-Snow et al. (2017[90]) provide evidence that radial highways decentralise service sector activity in Chinese cities, radial railroads decentralise industrial activity and ring roads decentralise both. This decentralisation pattern is similar to the one observed for European and US cities from the 1940s to the 1960s, during which time manufacturing plants originally located in central cities benefitted from the development of transport network and moved to the urban periphery to find lower labour and land costs (Mayer and Trevien, 2017[85]).

An important misconception is that transport infrastructure investment relieves congestion. The amount of vehicle-travelled kilometres in US cities increases proportionally to roadway lane kilometres for interstate highways (Duranton and Turner, 2011[94]). The results point to a "fundamental law of road congestion", i.e. more supply of roads leads to more people driving and the same level of congestion as before. Policymakers that aim at expanding the transport infrastructure network in order to reduce road congestion should keep in mind that as the network expands, more workers and firms will take advantage of it for their purposes, whether it is to commute to work or to ship goods, therefore leaving road congestion overall unchanged.

References

Adler, M. et al. (2020), "Roads, market access and regional economic development", *OECD Regional Development Working Papers*, OECD Publishing, Paris.   [53]

Aghion, P. and U. Akcigit (2015), *Innovation and Growth: The Schumpeterian Perspective*.   [62]

Agrawal, A., A. Galasso and A. Oettl (2017), "Roads and innovation", *The Review of Economics and Statistics*, Vol. 99/3, pp. 417-434.   [61]

Ahlfeldt, G. and A. Feddersen (2018), "From periphery to core: Measuring agglomeration effects using high-speed rail", *Journal of Economic Geography*, Vol. 18/2, pp. 355-390.   [68]

Ahlfeldt, G. et al. (2015), "The economics of density: Evidence from the Berlin Wall", *Econometrica*, Vol. 83/6, pp. 2127-2189. [84]

Ahrend, R. et al. (2014), "What Makes Cities More Productive? Evidence on the Role of Urban Governance from Five OECD Countries", *OECD Productivity Working Papers*, No. 6, OECD Publishing, Paris, https://doi.org/10.1787/2ce4b893-en. [77]

Albalate, D. and G. Bel (2012), "High-speed rail: Lessons for policy makers from experiences abroad", *Public Administration Review*, Vol. 72/3, pp. 336-349. [70]

Allain-Dupré, D., C. Hulbert and M. Vincent (2017), "Subnational Infrastructure Investment in OECD Countries: Trends and Key Governance Levers", *OECD Regional Development Working Papers*, No. 2017/05, OECD Publishing, Paris, https://dx.doi.org/10.1787/e9077df7-en. [12]

Atack, J. et al. (2010), "Did railroads induce or follow economic growth?: Urbanization and population growth in the American Midwest 1850-1860", *Social Science History*, Vol. 34/2, pp. 171–197. [64]

Audretsch, D., D. Dohse and J. Pereira dos Santos (2017), *Do Toll-free Highways Foster Firm Formation and Employment Growth? Results from a Quasi-natural Experiment*. [57]

Bailey, M. et al. (2019), *Social Connectedness in Urban Areas*. [89]

Baum-Snow, N. (2007), "Did highways cause suburbanization?", *The Quarterly Journal of Economics*, Vol. 122/2, pp. 775-805. [102]

Baum-Snow, N. et al. (2017), "Roads, railroads, and decentralization of Chinese cities", *Review of Economics and Statistics*, Vol. 99/3, pp. 435-448. [90]

Baum-Snow, N. et al. (2016), "Highways, market access, and urban growth in China". [17]

Berger, T. and K. Enflo (2015), "Locomotives of local growth: The short-and long-term impact of railroads in Sweden", *Journal of Urban Economics*, Vol. 98, pp. 124-138. [65]

Bernard, A., A. Moxnes and Y. Saito (2019), *Production Networks, Geography and Firm Performance*. [35]

Billings, S. (2011), "Estimating the value of a new transit option", *Regional Science and Urban Economics*, Vol. 41/6, pp. 525-536. [83]

Brandily, P. and F. Rauch (2018), *Roads and Urban Growth*. [92]

Broda, C. and D. Weinstein (2006), "Globalization and the gains from variety", *Quarterly Journal of Economics*, Vol. 121/2, pp. 541–585. [50]

Brookings Institution (2019), "Shifting into an era of repair: US infrastructure spending trends", https://www.brookings.edu/research/shifting-into-an-era-of-repair-us-infrastructure-spending-trends/. [39]

Brooks, L. and Z. Liscow (2019), "Infrastructure costs", *Hutchins Center Working Paper*, No. 54, Brookings. [7]

Büchel, K. and S. Kyburz (2016), *Fast Track to Growth? The Impact of Railway Access on Regional Economic Development in 19th Century Switzerland*. [66]

Carbo, J. et al. (2019), "Evaluating the causal economic impacts of transport investments: Evidence from the Madrid-Barcelona high speed rail corridor", *Journal of Applied Statistics*, Vol. 46/9, pp. 1714-1723. [69]

CEB (2017), *Investing in Public Infrastructure in Europe - A Local Economy Perspective*, Council of Europe Development Bank, https://coebank.org/media/documents/Investing_in_Public_Infrastructure_in_Europe_27dc1P g.pdf. [6]

Cervero, R. and C. Kang (2011), "Bus rapid transit impacts on land uses and land values in Seoul, Korea", *Transport Policy*, Vol. 18/1, pp. 102-116. [86]

Chandra, A. and E. Thompson (2000), "Does public infrastructure affect economic activity? Evidence from the rural interstate highway system". [59]

Combes, P. et al. (2012), "The productivity advantages of large cities: Distinguishing agglomeration from firm selection", *Econometrica*, Vol. 80/6, pp. 2543-2594. [78]

Combes, P., L. Gobillon and M. Lafourcade (2019), *Labour Productivity Gains from the "Greater Paris Express" Rail Project*. [72]

Combes, P. and M. Lafourcade (2005), "Transport costs: Measures, determinants, and regional policy implications for France", *Journal of Economic Geography*, Vol. 5, pp. 319-349. [49]

Crescenzi, R. and A. Rodríguez-Pose (2008), "Infrastructure endowment and investment as determinants of regional growth in the European Union: The economics of regional transport investment", *European Investment Bank Papers*, Vol. 13/2, pp. 62-101. [103]

Donaldson, D. and R. Hornbeck (2015), "Railroads and American economic growth: A market access approach". [67]

Duranton, G. and E. Guerra (2016), "Urban accessibility: Balancing land use and transportation", University of Pennsylvania, https://faculty.wharton.upenn.edu/wp-content/uploads/2017/05/Urban-accessibility-Balancing-land-use-and-transportation-Gilles.pdf (accessed on 3 April 2018). [22]

Duranton, G. et al. (2015), *Handbook of Regional and Urban Economics*, Elsevier. [97]

Duranton, G., P. Morrow and M. Turner (2014), "Roads and trade: Evidence from the US", *The Review of Economic Studies*, Vol. 81/2, pp. 681-724. [96]

Duranton, G. and M. Turner (2012), "Urban growth and transportation". [91]

Duranton, G. and M. Turner (2011), "The fundamental law of road congestion: Evidence from US cities", *American Economic Review*, Vol. 101/6, pp. 2616-2652. [94]

EC (2017), *Delivering TEN-T Facts and Figures*, European Commission. [30]

EC (2017), *Progress Report on the Implementation of the TEN-T Network in 2014 and 2015*, European Commission. [31]

EC (2014), *Guide to Cost-Benefit Analysis of Investment Projects*, European Commission. [24]

EC (n.d.), *Infrastructure and Investment*, European Commission, https://ec.europa.eu/transport/themes/infrastructure_en. [33]

European Parliament Research Service (2018), *Investment in Infrastructure in the EU: Gaps, Challenges, and Opportunities*. [20]

Eurostat (2020), *Railway Transport – Length of Lines, by Maximum Speed (rail_if_line_sp) (database)*. [34]

Fernald, J. (1999), "Roads to prosperity? Assessing the link between public capital and productivity", *The American Economic Review*, Vol. 89/3, pp. 619–638. [95]

Fretz, S., R. Parchet and F. Robert-Nicoud (2017), *Highways, Market Access and Spatial Sorting*. [75]

Furusawa, T. et al. (2017), "Global sourcing and domestic production networks", *CESifo Working Papers*, No. 6658, CESifo. [51]

Garcia-López, M., C. Hémet and E. Viladecans-Marsal (2017), "Next train to the polycentric city: The effect of railroads on subcenter formation", *Regional Science and Urban Economics*, Vol. 67, pp. 50-63. [93]

Garcia-López, M., A. Holl and E. Viladecans-Marsal (2015), "Suburbanization and highways in Spain when the Romans and the Bourbons still shape its cities", *Journal of Urban Economics*, Vol. 85, pp. 52-67. [104]

GETLINK (2019), *Traffic Figures*, https://www.getlinkgroup.com/uk/eurotunnel-group/operations/traffic-figures/. [5]

Ghani, E., A. Goswami and W. Kerr (2016), "Highway to success: The impact of the Golden Quadrilateral Project for the location and performance of Indian manufacturing", *The Economic Journal*, Vol. 126/591, pp. 317-357. [60]

Gibbons, S., S. Heblich and E. Pinchbeck (2019), *The Spatial Impacts of a Massive Rail Disinvestment Program: The Beeching Axe*. [71]

Gibbons, S. et al. (2019), "New road infrastructure: The effects on firms", *Journal of Urban Economics*, Vol. 110, pp. 35-50. [54]

Gibbons, S. and S. Machin (2004), *Valuing Rail Access Using Transport Innovations*. [81]

Gibbons, S., H. Overman and G. Resend (2011), "Real earnings disparities in Britain". [79]

Glaeser, E., M. Kahn and J. Rappaport (2008), "Why do the poor live in cities? The role of public transportation", *Journal of Urban Economics*, Vol. 63/1, pp. 1-24. [88]

Government of Canada (2020), *Transportation Activity Indicators, Transport Canada*, https://www150.statcan.gc.ca/t1/tbl1/en/tv.action?pid=2310026901&cubeTimeFrame.startMonth=01&cubeTimeFrame.startYear=2019&cubeTimeFrame.endMonth=07&cubeTimeFrame.endYear=2020&referencePeriods=20190101%2C20200701 (accessed on 4 November 2020). [99]

Greater London Authority (2018), *Mayor's Transport Strategy*, http://www.london.gov.uk (accessed on 15 July 2019). [23]

Holl, A. (2007), "Twenty years of accessibility improvements. The case of the Spanish motorway building programme", *Journal of Transport Geography*, Vol. 15/4, pp. 286-297. [52]

Holl, A. (2004), "Manufacturing location and impacts of road transport infrastructure: Empirical evidence from Spain", *Regional Science and Urban Economics*, Vol. 34/3, pp. 341-363. [55]

Holl, A. (2004), "Transport infrastructure, agglomeration economies and firm birth: Empirical evidence from Portugal", *Journal of Regional Science*, Vol. 44/4, pp. 693-712. [56]

Hornung, E. (2015), "Railroads and growth in Prussia", *Journal of the European Economic Association*, Vol. 13/4, pp. 699-736. [63]

IEA (2019), *The Future of Rail*, International Energy Agency, Paris, https://www.iea.org/reports/the-future-of-rail (accessed on 3 June 2020). [28]

IMF (2014), *IMF World Economic Outlook (WEO), Legacies, Clouds, Uncertainties*, International Monetary Fund, https://www.imf.org/external/pubs/ft/weo/2014/02/ (accessed on 5 September 2019). [15]

Institut d'Aménagement et d'Urbanisme (2013), *Perspectives d'accès ferroviaire aux pôles franciliens depuis le Bassin Parisien*. [36]

ITF (2019), *High Capacity Transport: Towards Efficient, Safe and Sustainable Road Freight*, International Transport Forum, OECD, Paris. [21]

ITF (2019), *ITF Transport Infrastructure Database*, International Transport Forum, OECD, Paris, https://doi.org/10.1787/trsprt-data-en (accessed on 29 July 2019). [8]

ITF (2019), *ITF Transport Outlook 2019*, OECD Publishing, Paris, https://doi.org/10.1787/transp_outlook-en-2019-en. [27]

ITF (2018), *Policies to Extend the Life of Road Assets*, International Transport Forum, OECD, Paris. [42]

ITF (2018), *Safer Roads with Automated Vehicles?*, International Transport Forum, OECD, Paris. [44]

ITF (2018), *Towards Road Freight Decarbonisation: Trends, Measure and Policies*, International Transport Forum, OECD, Paris. [43]

ITF (2017), *ITF Transport Outlook 2017*, OECD Publishing, Paris, http://dx.doi.org/10.1787/9789282108000-en. [47]

ITF (2014), *The Economics of Investment in High-Speed Rail*, ITF Round Tables, No. 155, OECD Publishing, Paris, https://dx.doi.org/10.1787/9789282107751-en. [29]

Kahn, M. (2007), "Gentrification trends in new transit-oriented communities: Evidence from 14 cities that expanded and built rail transit systems", *Real Estate Economics*, Vol. 35/2, pp. 155-182. [87]

Lee, N. and A. Lembcke (2020), "The economic benefits of accessibility: A survey", Unpublished Manuscript. [46]

Martí-Henneberg, J. (2013), "European integration and national models for railway networks (1840-2010)", *Journal of Transport Geography*. [48]

Mayer, T. and C. Trevien (2017), "The impact of urban public transportation evidence from the Paris region", *Journal of Urban Economics*, Vol. 102, pp. 1-21. [85]

McKinsey & Company (2016), *Bridging Global Infrastructure Gaps*.   [10]

McKinsey & Company (2013), "Infrastructure productivity: How to save $1 trillion a year".   [40]

Michaels, G. (2008), "The effect of trade on the demand for skill: Evidence from the interstate   [76]
highway system".

OECD (2020), "Building back better: A sustainable, resilient recovery after COVID-19", *Tackling*   [11]
Coronavirus (COVID-19): Contributing to a Global Effort, OECD, Paris,
http://www.oecd.org/coronavirus/policy-responses/building-back-better-a-sustainable-
resilient-recovery-after-covid-19-52b869f5/ (accessed on 10 June 2020).

OECD (2020), *Improving Transport Planning for Accessible Cities*, OECD Urban Studies, OECD   [45]
Publishing, Paris, https://dx.doi.org/10.1787/fcb2eae0-en.

OECD (2019), *Accelerating Climate Action: Refocusing Policies Through a Well-Being Lens -*   [37]
Highlights, OECD, Paris.

OECD (2019), *Accelerating Climate Action: Refocusing Policies through a Well-being Lens*,   [19]
OECD Publishing, Paris, https://dx.doi.org/10.1787/2f4c8c9a-en.

OECD (2019), *Regional Outlook 2019: Leveraging Megatrends for Cities and Rural Areas*,   [18]
OECD Publishing, Paris, https://doi.org/10.1787/9789264312838-en.

OECD (2018), *Maintaining the Momentum of Decentralisation in Ukraine*, OECD Multi-level   [25]
Governance Studies, OECD Publishing, Paris, https://dx.doi.org/10.1787/9789264301436-en.

OECD (2018), *OECD Territorial Reviews: The Megaregion of Western Scandinavia*, OECD   [38]
Publishing, Paris, http://dx.doi.org/10.1787/9789264290679-en.

OECD (2017), *Gaps and Governance Standards of Public Infrastructure in Chile: Infrastructure*   [2]
Governance Review, OECD Publishing, Paris, https://doi.org/10.1787/9789264278875-en.

OECD (2016), *OECD Regional Outlook 2016: Productive Regions for Inclusive Societies*, OECD   [41]
Publishing, Paris, https://doi.org/10.1787/9789264260245-en.

OECD (2016), *OECD Territorial Reviews: Japan 2016*, OECD Publishing, Paris,   [4]
http://dx.doi.org/10.1787/9789264250543-en.

OECD (2016), *Road Infrastructure, Inclusive Development and Traffic Safety in Korea*, OECD   [3]
Publishing, Paris, http://dx.doi.org/10.1787/9789264255517-en.

OECD (2015), "Chicago, United States", in *Governing the City*, OECD Publishing, Paris,   [14]
https://dx.doi.org/10.1787/9789264226500-9-en.

OECD (2015), *OECD Urban Policy Reviews: Mexico 2015: Transforming Urban Policy and*   [80]
Housing Finance, OECD Urban Policy Reviews, OECD Publishing, Paris,
https://doi.org/10.1787/9789264227293-en.

OECD (2012), *OECD Territorial Reviews: The Chicago Tri-State Metropolitan Area, United*   [13]
States 2012, OECD Territorial Reviews, OECD Publishing, Paris,
https://dx.doi.org/10.1787/9789264170315-en.

OECD/European Commission (2020), *Cities in the World: A New Perspective on Urbanisation*,   [101]
OECD Urban Studies, OECD Publishing, Paris, https://doi.org/10.1787/d0efcbda-en.

Pogonyi, C., D. Graham and J. Carbo (2019), "Metros, agglomeration and firm productivity. Evidence from London", *SSRN Electronic Journal*. [82]

Puga, D. (2002), "Progress report on the implementation of the TEN-T Network in 2014 and 2015", *Journal of Economic Geography*, Vol. 2, pp. 373-406. [32]

Redding, S. and M. Turner (2015), "Transportation costs and the spatial organization of economic activity", in *Handbook of Regional and Urban Economics*, Elsevier B.V. [105]

Sanchis-Guarner, R. (2012), *Driving up Wages: The Effects of Road Construction in Great Britain*. [58]

Stelder, D. (2016), "Regional accessibility trends in Europe: Road infrastructure, 1957-2012", *Regional Studies*, Vol. 50/6, pp. 983-995. [26]

Storeygard, A. (2016), "Farther on down the road: Transport costs, trade and urban growth in Sub-Saharan Africa", *The Review of Economic Studies*, Vol. 83/3, pp. 1263-1295. [106]

Transport Analysis (n.d.), "Transport indicators week 45", https://www.trafa.se/en/pages/transport-indicators/ (accessed on 4 November 2020). [100]

UK Government (2020), *Transport Use during the Coronavirus (COVID-19) Pandemic*, https://www.gov.uk/government/statistics/transport-use-during-the-coronavirus-covid-19-pandemic (accessed on 3 November 2020). [98]

UNECE (2016), "Infrastructure and growth", *Sustainable Development Brief*, No. 3, http://www.unece.org/?i (accessed on 5 September 2019). [16]

Venables, A., J. Laird and H. Overman (2014), "Transport investment and economic performance: Implications for project appraisal". [73]

Vickerman, R., K. Spiekermann and M. Wegener (1999), "Accessibility and economic development in Europe", *Regional Studies*, Vol. 33/1, pp. 1-15, http://dx.doi.org/10.1080/00343409950118878. [74]

World Bank (2018), *Belt and Road Initiative*, https://www.worldbank.org/en/topic/regional-integration/brief/belt-and-road-initiative. [9]

World Economic Forum (2016), *The Global Competitiveness Report 2016-2017*, World Economic Forum, Geneva, http://www3.weforum.org/docs/GCR2016-2017/05FullReport/TheGlobalCompetitivenessReport2016-2017_FINAL.pdf (accessed on 5 September 2019). [1]

Notes

[1] As a consequence of the increasing opportunities for trade and pressure on scarce resources, the construction of the railroad network in the United States led to a 60% increase in the value of agricultural land (Donaldson and Hornbeck, 2015[67]).

[2] Other than passenger traffic, the Channel tunnel has also eased freight traffic. More than one-quarter of total trade in goods between the UK and continental Europe goes through the Channel tunnel, which therefore functions as one of the main arteries for the exchange of goods in Europe.

[3] The term productivity spill-overs refers to the diffusion of partially non-excludable knowledge among neighbouring firms that interact by means of supply agreements, participation in formal and informal business community gatherings, etc. See further the section on benefits from road and rail infrastructure for a broader description of the positive externalities resulting from agglomeration.

[4] The analysis presented in this report on interregional transport infrastructure focuses on inland transport, in great part accounted for by rail and road transport. It therefore excludes transport via maritime ports and airports.

[5] Total inland infrastructure investment and maintenance spending includes road and rail transport. Calculations based on ITF (2019[8]).

[6] The European Regional Development Fund (ERDF) and the Cohesion Fund (CF) are the two main arms of EU Regional Policy. The ERDF aims to strengthen economic and social cohesion in the European Union by correcting imbalances between its regions and therefore involves all EU regions. On the other hand, the CF, whose goal is also to reduce economic and social disparities and promote sustainable development, is aimed at member states whose gross national income (GNI) per inhabitant is less than 90% of the EU average (https://ec.europa.eu/regional_policy/en/policy/what/investment-policy/). For information on how the funds are allocated, see https://cohesiondata.ec.europa.eu/overview.

[7] The proportion of the world population living in cities of at least 50 000 inhabitants has increased from 37% to 48% during 1975-2015 (OECD/European Commission, 2020[101]).

[8] This is also evident in the common global ambition set out in the Sustainable Development Goals that are part of the 2030 Agenda for Sustainable Development. Seven out of the 17 goals are transport-related (ITF, 2019[27]).

[9] Based on UK Government (2020[98]).

[10] The UK Department of Transport provides appraisals guidelines that recognise the importance of additional benefits accruing from the reorganisation of economic activity (Venables, Laird and Overman, 2014[73]), thus positioning itself as world leader in terms of the innovativeness of transport project appraisals.

[11] Based on Government of Canada (2020[99]).

[12] Based on Transport Analysis (n.d.[100]).

[13] Three assumptions guarantee the minimisation of the impact on total expenditure: i) costs preventing higher-capacity utilisation of the rail network are minimised; ii) revenues from rail system are maximised

(e.g. via land value capture systems); and iii) an effective system of taxes addressing environmental externalities is, in place.

[14] The empirical evidence is relatively scarce due primarily to the young age of many HS rail investment projects. See OECD (2018[38]) for a review of the existing evidence as part of the discussion on how HS rail investment could contribute to the integration of the megaregion of Western Scandinavia.

[15] The other important factors on which HS rail investment profitability typically rests in cost-benefit analyses are savings in construction costs and savings in travel time.

[16] See, for instance, Baum-Snow (2007[102]).

[17] Several recent papers summarise this literature (Redding and Turner, 2015[105]; Gibbons et al., 2019[54]).

[18] The studies include historic and contemporaneous infrastructure investments and were chosen for their application of empirical methods that allow the identification of causal effects. List of relevant studies in Annex Table 1.A.1.

[19] The slowdown in international trade in 2019-20 due to rising tariffs highlights this point. Rising bilateral tensions could reduce the global level of output by over 0.5% in 2020 (ITF, 2019[27]) relative to baseline OECD projections.

[20] As another example of the complementarity between transport infrastructure and other cost-reducing measures, looking at a set of 15 coastal Sub-Saharan countries, the 300% oil price increase between 2002 and 2008 induced the income of cities near the capital and port city to increase by 7% relative to otherwise identical cities 500 kilometres farther away (Storeygard, 2016[106]).

[21] The expected growth rate in market access given the growth rate in highway length refers to the growth rate in market access returned by a linear regression on the growth rate in highway length as unique regressor.

[22] Other studies confirming the positive impact on employment are (Audretsch, Dohse and Pereira dos Santos, 2017[57]; Duranton and Turner, 2012[91]).

[23] Data on population growth tend to be more easily available given the early period (second half of the 19th century) when most of these projects took place in developed countries.

[24] The Grand Paris Express is a group of rapid transit lines being built in the Île-de-France region, consisting of about 200 km and connecting 68 train stations.

[25] Baum-Snow (2007[102]) shows that each new highway caused central city population in US cities to decline by about 18% between 1950 and 1990. Garcia-López et al. (2015[104]) confirm the same findings for Spain, Baum-Snow et al. (2017[90]) for China and Fretz et al. (2017[75]) for Switzerland.

Annex 1.A. Literature

Annex Table 1.A.1. List of studies on the economic impact of interregional transport infrastructure investment

	Interregional transport	Type of infrastructure investment	Period
France	(Combes, Gobillon and Lafourcade, 2019[72])	Commuter train	To be realised
Germany	(Hornung, 2015[63])	Railway	1840-71
Germany	(Ahlfeldt and Feddersen, 2018[68])	High-speed railway	
Portugal	(Holl, 2004[56])	Highway	1986-97
Portugal	(Audretsch, Dohse and Pereira dos Santos, 2017[57])	Highway	2010-11
Spain	(Carbo et al., 2019[69])	High-speed railway	
Spain	(Holl, 2004[55])	Highway	1980-94
Sweden	(Berger and Enflo, 2015[65])	Railway	1855-70
Switzerland	(Fretz, Parchet and Robert-Nicoud, 2017[75])	Highway	1960-2010
Switzerland	(Büchel and Kyburz, 2016[66])	Railway	19th century
United Kingdom	(Sanchis-Guarner, 2012[58])	Highway	2002-08
United Kingdom	(Gibbons et al., 2019[54])	Highway	1997-2008
United States	(Fernald, 1999[95])	Highway	1953-89
United States	(Chandra and Thompson, 2000[59])	Highway	1969-93
United States	(Michaels, 2008[76])	Highway	1959-75
United States	(Atack et al., 2010[64])	Railway	1850-60
United States	(Duranton, Morrow and Turner, 2014[96])	Highway	2007
United States	(Donaldson and Hornbeck, 2015[67])	Railway	1870-90

Note: See Duranton, G. et al. (2015[97]), *Handbook of Regional and Urban Economics*, Elsevier, for a broader survey of the literature that includes a larger geographical scope.

2 Transport for access to opportunities in cities

This chapter discusses the role of transport for quality of life in cities and provides an analysis of how well local transport systems do in terms of connecting citizens with surrounding opportunities in different cities and for different socio-economic groups. It starts with a presentation of different channels through which transport policy matters for life in cities, most notably its role at fostering the transition towards a climate-neutral economy. Next, it moves to the description of how accessibility, i.e. the number of opportunities reachable from a given place in a given time by a given transport mode, and other transport quality indicators vary across cities of different countries and different sizes. It analyses the sizeable and positive accessibility gap between high- and low-income groups within cities and between cities in the same country. It concludes with potential explanations and suggested ways forward to improve accessibility inclusiveness in countries.

Transport investment contributes to quality of life in cities

The transport system provides access to economic opportunities and thereby enhances quality of life in cities. As established in Chapter 1, faster connections allow reaching a broader set of opportunities, e.g. jobs and services in a given time. In many cities, opportunities, such as jobs, are often concentrated in few places (typically the city centre). Faster connections from and to the city centre make higher job density in city centres more sustainable, thereby allowing cities to better reap the positive externalities associated with density.[1]

The transport system plays a critical role in making parts of the city viable places to build homes and create jobs. For example, investments in transport infrastructure in the metropolitan area of Vancouver have been credited as the force behind the reputation as one of the best places to live in Canada and the world. The problem is that as the built area and population grow, the number of challenges for the city also increases. For Vancouver, the boom in house prices and rents in central areas are pushing people to move to the suburbs where they do not always have the same level of access to opportunities.

Transport investment needs to keep up with growth in cities. Valle de México, the metropolitan area around Mexico's capital Mexico City experienced rapid population growth from the 1950s onwards. From the 1980s onwards, growth started to slow down. At the same time, the share of the population living in the poorly connected commuting zone has continued growing, thus causing rising congestion. To maintain growth, the transport system must catch up with the rapid development the metropolitan area has undergone in the last decades, crucially by connecting and densifying the commuting zone to turn it into a more attractive residential choice (OECD, 2015[1]). The planned expansion of the metropolitan area, in particular along transport corridors, i.e. transit-oriented development, is also crucial to alleviate the investment burden. As cities sprawl over increasingly larger areas, the cost of connecting the entire metropolitan area to (public) transport grows with significantly higher costs for infrastructure provision. In the United States, for example, the road network in low-density cities has is about three time as long (in terms of kilometres per capita) than in higher-density cities (Litman, 2015[2]).

By reducing car usage, investments in public transport also create the opportunity to convert parking into green and walkable space, another important driver of quality of life in cities (Leinberger and Alfonzo, 2012[3]). Investments in public transport give the opportunity for residents to be less car-dependent. If they succeed in making travellers switch from car to public transport, thereby reducing the demand for parking space, policymakers can next consider whether to convert the space previously occupied by parking into green, walkable and recreational areas, with positive implications for the well-being of residents. Alternatively, in less densely populated neighbourhoods, the new space can be used to expand the housing supply, therefore releasing potential upwards pressure on housing costs.

The most important factors that link transport and quality of life of residents differ across metropolitan areas. The transport vision for metropolitan areas like London, New York and Vancouver is to meet all transport needs in a way that enhances the health of residents, communities, the economy and the environment to maintain or even improve living standards. For New York City, United States, to sustain the city's growth and expand capacity, it is essential to allocate more street space to walking, biking and buses trying to move the greatest number of people while using the least amount of street capacity (NYC DOT, 2016[4]). London adopted the "Healthy Streets Approach" as part of its transport strategy. The basic premise is that the quality of the experience of using the city streets helps to define the quality of the journey. All metro and rail journeys rely on good street access to stations and streets, and are therefore important to providing attractive public transport options for each mode (Box 2.1).

Box 2.1. London's Healthy Streets Approach

In the United Kingdom, London's transport strategy has adopted a Healthy Streets Approach that provides the framework for putting human health and experience at the heart of city planning. It uses ten evidence-based indicators to assess the experience of being in the streets. Good performance on each indicator means that individual streets are appealing places to walk, cycle and spend time. Improvements against all indicators across the city's streets are expected to transform the day-to-day experience of living and working in London. The ten indicators are:

- *Clear air* – improving air quality.
- *Pedestrians from all walks of life* – streets should be welcoming places for everyone to walk and spend time.
- *Easy to cross* – to encourage walking and connect communities.
- *Shade and shelter* – to enable everybody to use the streets whatever the weather.
- *Places to stop and rest* – to foster mobility for all groups of people.
- *Not too noisy* – to improve the ambience of the street environments encouraging travel and human interaction.
- *People choose to walk, cycle and use public transport* – walking and cycling are the healthiest and most sustainable ways of travel. A successful transport system encourages and enables more people to walk and cycle more often and this is achieved by reducing motor traffic and improving the experience of being in the street.
- *People feel safe* – people should not feel worried about road danger or experience threats to their personal safety.
- *Things to see and so* – people are more likely to use the streets when their journey is interesting and stimulating with attractive views, buildings, plantings and where other people are using the street.
- *People feel relaxed* – streets are not dominated by motorised traffic, and pavements and cycle paths are not overcrowded, dirty, cluttered or in disrepair.

Source: Greater London Authority (2018[5]), *Mayor's Transport Strategy*, http://www.london.gov.uk (accessed on 15 July 2019).

The New York City Strategic Plan intends to improve street safety as part of its transport strategy. The plan considers the streets as conduits for people and goods as well as public spaces essential to the life and vibrancy of the city. Its basic premise is that the more attractive the streets and sidewalks, the more pedestrians will choose to use them (NYC DOT, 2016[4]). Streets make up 27% of New York City's land area and, for many residents, the local street is also their backyard. Therefore, the transport strategy aims to: "make streets and sidewalks attractive safe public spaces for walking, resting and gathering; expand public open space by creating pedestrian plazas across the five boroughs, especially in underserved neighbourhoods; [and] reconnect communities and create new open spaces by enhancing and activating underutilised areas under bridges, elevated roads and train lines" (NYC DOT, 2016, p. 59[4]). Improving the open space and reconnecting communities is a way to encourage more social cohesion and urban redevelopment around transport.

Through improving access to green spaces, cities and communities can contribute to the United Nations (UN) Sustainable Development Goals (SDGs) (OECD, 2020[6]). In SDG 11.7, the global agenda to sustainably improve living standards and the quality of life across the developed and developing world includes an explicit target for access to green space. Green areas are an important amenity for local residents, especially if reachable within a short walk or ride. The likelihood of being able to reach within a short walk a green area in cities is however inversely proportional to average urban density. For instance, the metropolitan area of Paris is on average more densely developed than the metropolitan area of Rome, thus making it easier for its residents to get to work in relatively little time (see the upcoming section on this). However, people living in Rome's densest areas have access on average to 15% more square metres than people living in Paris' densest areas, which is approximately a third of the variation in going from an area in central Paris with low-to-intermediate access to green areas to one with intermediate-to-high access (Figure 2.1). A third urban development model, alternative to the one of Paris and Rome, exists and it consists of reconciling efficient development and sustainability within the same urban space.

Box 2.2. New York City's Plaza Equity Program

The New York City (NYC) Department of Transportation (DOT) focuses on improving sidewalks and streets but also on creating signature open spaces across the five boroughs, particularly in areas with few open space resources. Through the *NYC Plaza Program*, DOT partners with local communities to convert underused streets into public plazas. According to the strategic plan, a well-designed plaza provides residents with a place to gather, promotes local business, reconnects neighbourhoods and creates a venue for recreational and cultural events. Thus, the DOT provides financial assistance to plaza partners in low- and moderate-income areas. The DOT is also exploring ways to activate and beautify areas under elevated highways and train lines. The aim is to ensure that residents live within a 10-minute walk of a quality open space.

To date, the DOT has developed or is planning 73 plazas across the 5 boroughs. The problem is that not every community has a partner organisation that can afford the required upkeep a public plaza demands. That is why the Plaza Equity Program provides USD 1.4 million in technical assistance for designated medium- and high-need plazas citywide. The programme provides funding to under-resourced communities to support their plazas, providing needed funds for maintenance services, including daily cleaning, trash removal, furniture management and horticultural care. Partner organisations also receive technical assistance with navigating city permitting processes, maintenance and event planning. Of the 73 plazas throughout the city, 30 receive support, enabling these diverse communities to have a high-quality public space.

Source: NYC DOT (2016[4]), *New York City Strategic Plan 2016*, https://www.nycdotplan.nyc/PDF/Strategic-plan-2016.pdf (accessed on 6 August 2019).

From mobility to accessibility

Quality of life in cities depends on accessibility not mobility. For decades transport investment aimed to increase the number of travellers and speed up their trips. This allowed cities to grow as people could commute longer distances in a shorter time. In Korea, for example, the average commute was less than 10 kilometres one way and took 42 minutes in 1990. Twenty years later it was 13 kilometres in only 32 minutes (OECD, 2016[7]). A focus on passenger number and speeds meant that transport became an end in itself rather than a means to access jobs, friends, family, amenities, etc. The concept of "accessibility" acknowledges that it is the access to opportunities that transport provides that matters for people's well-being and the functioning of cities. "Accessibility" denotes the opportunities that a resident of a city can reach using different modes of transport within a given time, where opportunities can include access to people, jobs, shops, services, green spaces, restaurants, etc. In practice, measures of accessibility tend to be limited by the need for very granular data on opportunities (see below on measurement).

Figure 2.1. How many square kilometres of green can be accessed from different parts of cities?

Paris   Rome

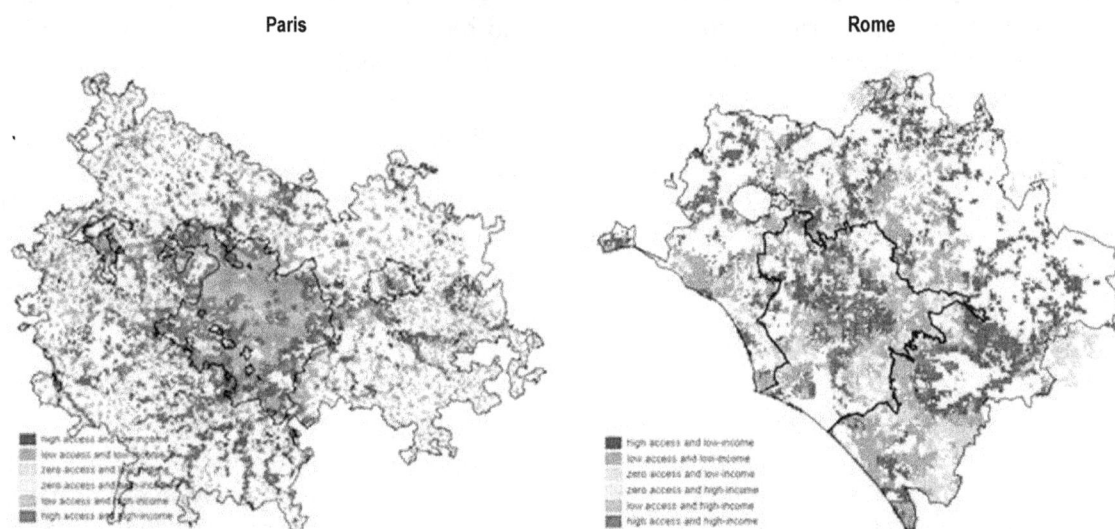

Note: Purple coloured cells correspond to cells with income below the city-specific median, where the median is population-weighted. Green coloured cells are those with income above. Darker coloured cells are those benefitting from better accessibility, light coloured ones the opposite, where the threshold is given by the overall city-specific median. Outer boundaries denote the functional urban area (FUA), inner ones the core of the FUA. See Annex Table 2.A.3 for a description of income data.
Source: Data on transport accessibility are from ITF (2019[8]), *Benchmarking Accessibility in Cities*, International Transport Forum, Paris.

The benefits of pursuing accessibility in cities

Accessibility contributes to broader government objectives of well-being and sustainability (ITF, 2019[9]). The provision of "access to safe, affordable, accessible and sustainable transport systems for all" features among the UN SDGs as a necessary step towards building sustainable cities and communities (OECD, 2020[6]). However, cities need to improve their understanding of the links between accessibility and well-being. Transport can contribute more effectively to wider well-being objectives. It enables access to jobs, education, healthcare, services, markets and other services and goods. It helps to improve quality of life and assists in lifting people out of poverty. Nevertheless, this can only be achieved if the potential synergies between improving the access to goods, services and information, and goals such as environmental protection, limiting social exclusion and improving health are considered (ITF, 2019[9]).

A focus on mobility rather than accessibility may lead to long commutes, mobility divides, air pollution and loss of public space. The success of transport infrastructure investment is often judged by the volume of use of the infrastructures. Such a focus on mobility rather than on the access to opportunities that transport provides can come at the cost of significant negative externalities. They incentivise more traffic and longer trips, thereby creating pollution that could have been avoided. The space used for infrastructures is "lost" for alternative uses. Therefore, to promote sustainable accessibility, cities are increasingly adopting policies that endorse nearness, densification, mixed land uses, integration and slow transport modes to redefine planning. In countries like Sweden, accessibility and sustainability are the principal policy goals of urban development at the national and subnational levels of government (Gil Solá, Vilhelmson and Larsson, 2018[10]). Gothenburg is pursuing a traffic strategy that promotes slower transport modes and local living (Hellberg et al., 2014[11]); Stockholm is planning for future urban development in terms of a compact city (City of Stockholm, n.d.[12]); and Malmö aims to be a city of short distances (City of Malmö, 2016[13]).

Accessibility may also be a channel for cities to address global challenges such as climate change. Approximately 10 billion trips are made every day in urban areas around the world and a significant share of these trips are high-carbon and energy-intensive private motorised vehicles (Rode et al., 2014[14]). According to the Intergovernmental Panel on Climate Change (IPCC) (2014[15]), about 80% of the increase in global transport emissions since 1970 has been due to road vehicles. Around 10% of the global population account for 80% of total motorised passenger-kilometres, which means that most of the world population hardly contributes to emissions at all. OECD countries dominate transport emissions of greenhouse gases (GHG) but emissions in Asian countries are rapidly increasing (IPCC, 2014[15]). Nowadays, planners and researchers focus on compact, transit-accessible, pedestrian-oriented, mixed-use development patterns and land reuse issues to foster smart growth and urban sustainable development. In Sweden, for instance, work on a total transport system is expected to increase by 29% between 2010 and 2030. In the metropolitan area of Gothenburg, the use of private car will stand at around 25% by 2030; therefore, to achieve climate objectives, total passenger volumes need to be reduced by 20% (from 2010 levels) by 2030 (Hellberg et al., 2014[11]).

Transport authorities and city planners acknowledge the relevance of transport in socio-economic development and environmental protection. Investment in rail, buses, cycling and walking links to goods and services intend to use traffic to boost cities' growth potential. For that, cities require providing high-quality public transport services that connect seamlessly to other forms of travel to provide alternatives to car use. The experience of cities like London, Malmö, Prague and Vancouver suggests that getting the planning process right is key to making transport a key contributor to sustainable and inclusive growth. In the aftermath of the current COVID-19 crisis, there will be opportunities to reallocate road space and encourage active transport to support the transition towards carbon neutrality and boost healthy lifestyles. At least 150 cities around the world have taken action during 2020 to create temporary cycle lanes and other spaces for active transport that allow travellers to maintain a social distance judged safe with respect to the transmission of the virus (ITF, 2020[16]).

Accessibility is also a factor that may contribute to the city's competitiveness. Cities and regions compete for students and skilled workers to join the labour force. Accessibility to surrounding areas and attractive urban environments are important factors for maintaining and attracting a skilled workforce.

Measuring access to opportunities

Access to opportunities – henceforth "accessibility" – builds on two elements: the presence of a transport system and the opportunities the transport system gives access to. The simple existence of a public transport stop, for instance, does not translate into good access to opportunities if few jobs or services can be reached via a given public transport connection. Accessibility-based indicators therefore represent an improvement with respect to the existing metrics that were used to gauge the magnitude of benefits from transport infrastructure and that tended to be based uniquely on the first element, i.e. the possibility of accessing the transport network from a given place. Despite growing recognition of the necessity to adopt accessibility-based measures as a guiding element of local policymaking, the paucity of accessibility-based decision-making frameworks hinders their use in urban and regional planning. The Urban Access Framework developed by the OECD in co-operation with the European Commission (EC) and the International Transport Forum (ITF) represents a first important step towards filling this gap (ITF, 2019[8]).

The Urban Access Framework jointly developed by the EC, the ITF and the OECD describes the access to opportunities provided by the urban transport network (ITF, 2019[8]). The framework provides three easy to interpret measures for accessibility and its links with the performance of the transport network at the city level. The measures are calculated based on the existing transport network and all potential travel from any point in a city to any other point. The Urban Access Framework has allowed the creation of harmonised indicators across a large set of European metropolitan areas. These indicators are flexible with respect to the choice of geography (i.e. what is "urban") and can be easily combined with external sources of data. For different transport modes, such as driving, cycling, walking or public transport, the framework includes three indicators: accessibility, proximity and transport performance.

- Accessibility refers to the total number of destinations that can be reached from a given location by driving, cycling, walking or taking public transport within a given amount of time. It is shaped by both the availability of opportunities in the surroundings of the given location and the characteristics of the transport network connecting that location to other parts of the city.

- Proximity is defined as the total number of destinations available within a given distance from a given location regardless of the travel time required to access them.

- Performance of the transport network captures how well the network connects residents of a given area to the opportunities existing in the proximity of such an area. It compares the total number of destinations reachable from a given location by a given transport mode within a given amount of time with the total number of destinations available within a given distance.

How many shops can residents access within 30 minutes?

Accessibility indicators implementing the EC-ITF-OECD Urban Access Framework are available for 121 European metropolitan areas for 2018 (Box 2.3). For four countries (France, England [UK], Italy and Spain), accessibility indicators are matched with data on income (or a proxy thereof) at the neighbourhood level (Annex Table 2.A.3). This combination of data sources gives the opportunity to zoom into each city and assess who benefits from better access to opportunities. The focus of this chapter is on accessibility by car and public transport within a 30-minute ride time. Car and public transport accounted jointly for 96% of urban passenger transport in OECD countries in 2015 and 30 minutes is the length of the average daily commute in OECD countries, except for Japan and Korea (OECD, 2017[17]). The analysis focuses on consumption opportunities as captured by the number of shops people can reach from their place of residence. Shop accessibility was chosen because, among the opportunities included in the dataset, it is the one that is more likely to have a strong correlation with jobs accessibility. Unlike other opportunities, the location of shops and jobs alike is mostly market-driven. Policymakers have indeed fewer tools to influence the distribution of shops than they have, for example, with schools. In the case of public services, e.g. schools or hospitals, they can, for instance, improve accessibility, not only by intervening on the transport network but also through investments in either the creation of new facilities or the expansion of existing ones.

Box 2.3. The EC-ITF-OECD Urban Access Framework

The EC, the ITF and the OECD jointly developed the Urban Access Framework, which provides a flexible framework to capture accessibility and transport performance in cities.

According to the Urban Access Framework, accessibility is measured on a 500-by-500-metre grid and refers to the number of opportunities reachable within a fixed amount of time from a given grid cell through the available transport network. The measure has been calculated with respect to a large set of opportunities, i.e. other people, schools, hospitals, food shops, restaurants, recreational activities and green spaces. These indicators have been computed for 121 metropolitan areas in 30 European countries based on data for 2018 (although not all transport modes are available in all cities). In terms of data sources, opportunities have been identified based on either OpenStreetMap or proprietary data sources (e.g. TomTom).

Accessibility is itself shaped by two further characteristics of the urban space. The first is proximity, i.e. how many opportunities there exist within a fixed physical distance from a given location. The second is the performance of the transport network, defined as the ratio between the number of opportunities reachable within a given time and the number of opportunities existing in the proximity of

---

a given location. The higher this ratio, the more efficient the transport network, in the sense that it allows people to reach a larger share of the opportunities that exist nearby.

Figure 2.2 shows the distribution of accessibility, proximity and performance by car across the wider metropolitan area of Hamburg. Proximity (top left-hand figure) in Hamburg as well as in most cities in the sample is higher in the city centre compared to the commuting zone, due to the higher density typical of city centres. Conversely, performance (bottom figure) of the car transport network is higher in the commuting zone, due to the more intense traffic and lower speed limits in the city centre. Since accessibility increases in both proximity and performance, these two patterns represent two opposing forces. Ultimately, the differences in proximity between the centre and the commuting zone outweigh the differences in performance in the case of the city of Hamburg, so that accessibility is on average higher in the city centre compared to other parts of the cities (top right-hand figure).

Figure 2.2. Accessibility in the Metropolitan Area of Hamburg

Proximity, accessibility within 30-minute car ride and performance of the car transport network in Hamburg

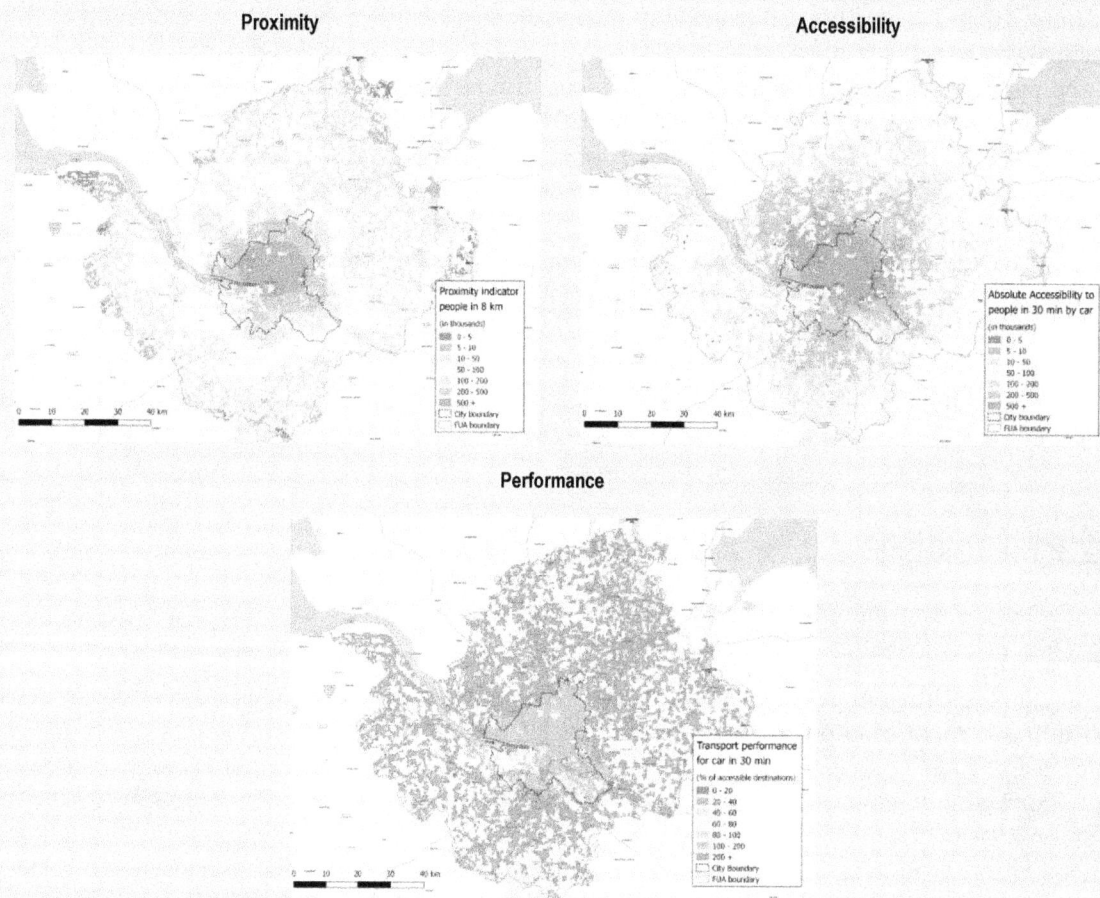

Source: ITF (2019[8]), *Benchmarking Accessibility in Cities*, International Transport Forum, Paris.

Across European metropolitan areas, average accessibility by car is higher than average accessibility by public transport. The average number of shops reachable within a 30-minute car ride is 1 402, more than twice the average number of shops reachable by public transport (Figure 2.3). Car accessibility is higher than public transport accessibility for access to public services as well. Across the 118 cities considered, the average number of schools accessible within a 30-minute car ride is 354 (Annex Figure 2.A.1). This number drops to 112 when considering public transport rides. A similar ranking between car and public transport accessibility is found for hospitals as well (Annex Figure 2.A.2). Residents of the cities considered can access, on average, 5 hospitals within a 30-minute public transport ride and as many as 17 within 30 minutes by car.

Figure 2.3. Number of shops reachable within a 30-minute ride across a set of FUAs, 2018

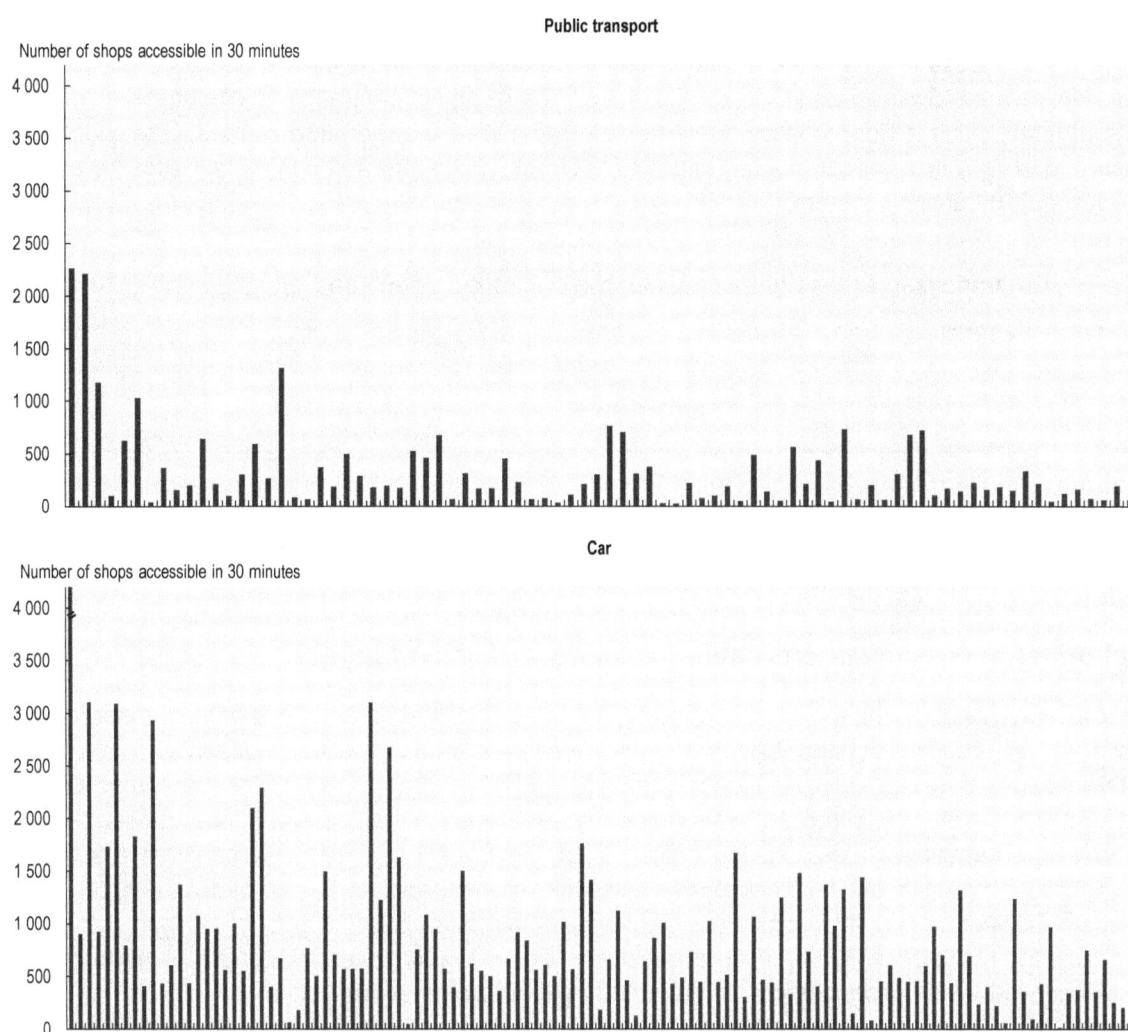

Note: Each bar corresponds to an FUA or city. The length of each bar corresponds to the average number of shops (for food) accessible within a 30-minute ride by public transport (upper panel) or by car (lower panel). Cities are sorted in descending order according to their total population. Average accessibility per city is calculated as a weighted average of cell-specific accessibility with weights given by the population residing in a cell relative to the total population. 118 metropolitan areas for car accessibility and 82 for public transport accessibility. See Annex Table 2.A.1 and Annex Table 2.A.2 for a list of the metropolitan areas included.
Source: Data on transport accessibility are from ITF (2019[8]), *Benchmarking Accessibility in Cities*, International Transport Forum, Paris.

Larger metropolitan areas provide better access to opportunities. Figure 2.3 reports the number of shops accessible within a 30-minute ride by car or public transport across European metropolitan areas. The largest metropolitan areas have significantly better access. In the sample, the 20 largest metropolitan areas provide access to more than 3 times the number of shops than the 20 smallest metropolitan areas for trips by car and nearly 3 times the number of shops for access by public transport.[2] A similar gradient along the city size hierarchy is present for public services as well.[3] Beyond the general tendency for better access in larger metropolitan areas, there is sizeable variation in the performance of metropolitan areas. Some smaller metropolitan areas provide access equal to that of mid-sized ones and the transport network in some of the largest metropolitan areas performs so badly that it provides access to the same number of opportunities offered to a resident in a much smaller metropolitan area.

Accessibility in the commuting zone is much lower than in city centres. Across 32 metropolitan areas in England, France, Italy and Spain, the number of shops reachable by car from the city centre is on average almost six times higher than for the commuting zone (Table 2.1). The ratio is as high as 23 for public transport. For access to jobs in the United Kingdom, accessibility in the commuting zone is much lower than in city centres (Swinney and Bidgood, 2014[18]).[4] The rising concentration of jobs observed in the city centre of many cities is likely to accentuate such a gap. Cities are therefore coming increasingly under pressure to build a more effective integration between the city centre and commuting zone by means of their local public transport system.

Table 2.1. Differences in accessibility between the commuting zone and the city centre, 2018

	Commuting zone	City centre	City centre/commuting zone ratio
Public transport	28	651	23.25
Car	281	1 617	5.95

Note: Each cell in the table reports the population-weighted number of shops accessible within a 30-minute ride by either public transport or car, across the city, in the city centre and commuting zone. The cities included are the 32 metropolitan areas located in England, France, Italy and Spain.
Source: Data on transport accessibility are from ITF (2019[8]), *Benchmarking Accessibility in Cities*, International Transport Forum, Paris.

What drives access to opportunities: Proximity or performance?

Accessibility depends on the proximity of opportunities as well as the performance of the transport system. "Proximity" captures that opportunities in cities are provided close to where people live (in other words, whether housing is developed close to jobs, shopping and other opportunities). The more opportunities in the vicinity of people, the more accessible the city – independent of how well the transport network functions. "Performance" relates to the efficiency of the transport network. It captures the share of opportunities in proximity of where people live and which can be reached by car, public transport, walking or cycling. For example, London offers excellent access to opportunities by public transport compared to other cities but ranks low in terms of car accessibility. This result is driven by the subpar performance of the road network – due to congestion – compared to the public transport system.

The performance of the road network tends to be better in small metropolitan areas compared to larger ones (Figure 2.4). For example, in metropolitan areas with more than 1 million inhabitants, residents can access, on average, the total number of opportunities available in an 8 km radius plus an additional 23% within a 30-minute car ride. In metropolitan areas with less than 1 million inhabitants, the additional number of opportunities is, on average, 42%. Congestion is partly responsible for the subpar performance of the road network in large cities compared to smaller ones (ITF, 2019[8]); a more extensive commuting zone is another reason.

Better accessibility in larger metropolitan areas is driven by greater proximity to opportunities for the average resident rather than the performance of the transport network. Overall, the greater proximity to opportunities in large cities outweighs the lower performance of their transport system, thus resulting in better accessibility. Larger cities tend to provide more opportunities in the proximity of the place where people live. Their greater density reduces travel time leading to overall more attractive cities where accessibility is higher not just in certain areas but overall. This is in contrast to metropolitan areas below 750 000 inhabitants. For them, the performance of the transport network is the key distinguishing feature. Large metropolitan areas have worse transport performance compared to other metropolitan areas when it comes to car transport relative to public transport networks. Congestion matters more for car use than for public transport. There are, however, exceptions. Milan, for example, is a rather sparsely populated metropolitan area, which attenuates the issue of road congestion and improves the performance of the road network. However, the city lacks an effective public transport network connecting its commuting zone to the city centre. As a result, Milan ranks lower in its public transport performance among the metropolitan areas than in its road network performance.

Figure 2.4. Proximity vs. performance as drivers of accessibility within cities, 2018

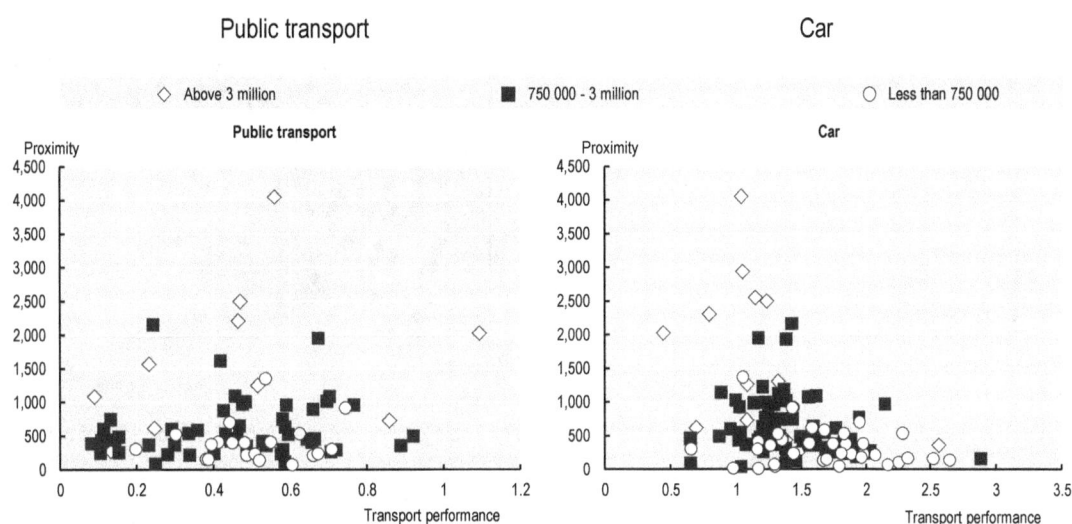

Note: The figure reports on the vertical axis of each panel the "proximity" of shops in a city, i.e. the average number of shops located within an 8 km radius; on the horizontal axis the average "performance" of the transport mode. Performance is measured as the ratio of the average (weighted by population) number of shops that can be reached within 30 minutes and the average (weighted by population) number of shops within an 8 km radius. Each dot corresponds to an FUA.
Source: Data on transport accessibility are from ITF (2019[8]), *Benchmarking Accessibility in Cities*, International Transport Forum, Paris.

Who benefits from better accessibility?

Even cities with the highest accessibility have pockets of better and worse access. The difference in accessibility for trips by car between the best-connected neighbourhoods – defined as the 500 m² grid cells with the highest accessibility in a metropolitan area that account for 25% of its population – and the worst-connected neighbourhoods (25% of the population with worst accessibility) ranges from just 1% (Saragossa, Spain) to nearly 7 times (670% in Gothenburg, Sweden).[5] On average across the 118 European metropolitan areas, the number of opportunities that can be reached by residents of best-connected neighbourhoods by car is more than 2.5 times higher than the one that can be reached by residents of worst-connected neighbourhoods.

Access to opportunities by car is more unequal in larger metropolitan areas. In small metropolitan areas with less than 565 000 inhabitants, the number of shops reachable within 30 minutes of driving by residents of best-connected neighbourhoods is on average 85% higher than the number of shops reachable by residents of worst-connected neighbourhoods. In large metropolitan areas with more than 3 million inhabitants, this number is as high as 380% (Figure 2.5).[6] Greater dispersion in car accessibility in larger metropolitan areas is driven by a few areas being characterised by extremely high as opposed to extremely low accessibility compared to the rest of the metropolitan area. In small metropolitan areas, the number of shops reachable within 30 minutes of driving by residents of best-connected neighbourhoods is on average 11% higher than the number of shops reachable from a neighbourhood with average accessibility. In large metropolitan areas, this number is almost 5 times larger and equal to 60%.

Figure 2.5. Transport accessibility inequality within European metropolitan areas, 2018

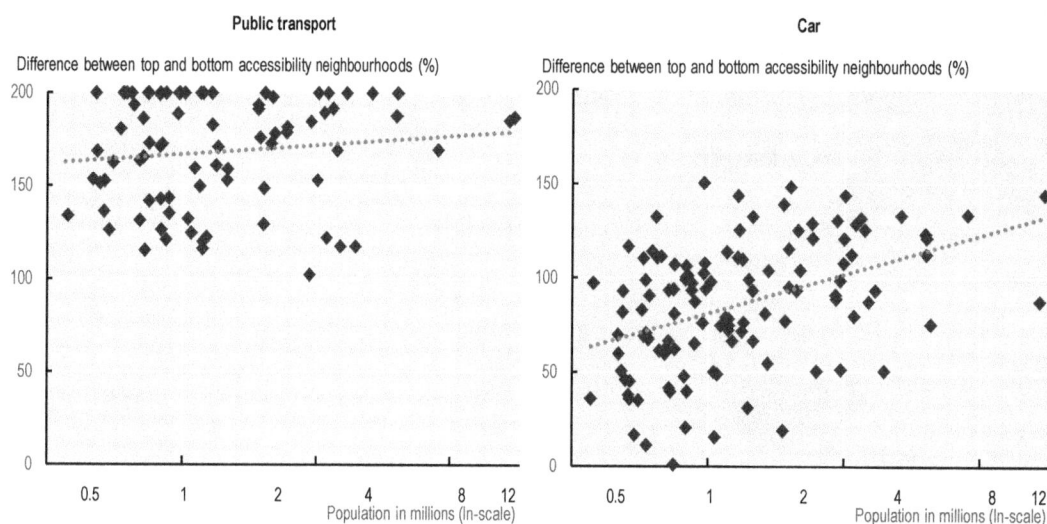

Note: Each dot represents 1 of 118 metropolitan areas in 2018. See Annex Table 2.A.1 and Annex Table 2.A.2 for a list of the metropolitan areas included. On the vertical axis, the difference between the 75th and 25th percentile of the population-weighted accessibility distribution across neighbourhoods in each given metropolitan area is plotted. For small differences, the number corresponds to the percentage difference between the 75th and 25th percentile. It is calculated as $difference = 100 \times 2(p(75) - p(25))/(p(75) + p(25))$, which allows to retain metropolitan areas for which the 25th percentile of the accessibility distribution is equal to 0. The "difference" indicator ranges from 0 to 200. On the horizontal axis, the logarithm of population is plotted.
Source: Data on transport accessibility are from ITF (2019[8]), *Benchmarking Accessibility in Cities*, International Transport Forum, Paris.

Greater dispersion in car accessibility for larger metropolitan areas is a by-product of a higher concentration of population in the city centre. Across the 118 metropolitan areas considered, a doubling in the number of residents is, on average, associated with a 5 percentage point increase in the share of people living in the city centre. Many of the 118 metropolitan areas have a gradient in accessibility with high accessibility in the city centre and a more or less smooth decline in accessibility as the distance from the city centre increases. If a large share of the population lives in the city centre, more people have access to a large number of shops within a short ride, thus giving rise to a larger gap between people residing in the city centre and people residing in the commuting zone.

Differences in accessibility by public transport are larger than for accessibility by car, but the difference depends less on city size (Figure 2.5). Twenty-one of the 82 European metropolitan areas with public transport data provide no access to shops within 30 minutes to at least 25% of the population in the metropolitan area. This is due to low public transport coverage of the population in the commuting zone. On average, the best-connected neighbourhoods provide access to 168% more shops via public transport than the worst-connected neighbourhoods. There is only a weak association with city size. Two factors compensating each other are behind this result. On the one hand, the number of opportunities reachable by public transport by residents of best-connected neighbourhoods is much higher in larger than in smaller cities; on the other, in small cities, a large share of the population lives in the commuting zone where public transport is often absent. These two factors tend to compensate each other, with the result that the dispersion of public transport accessibility across neighbourhoods is just as high in larger cities than in smaller ones.

Public transport uptake for the daily commute is positively associated with the effectiveness of the public transport system. An analysis based on a sample of 11 French metropolitan areas shows that workers living in neighbourhoods with better public transport performance, i.e. a larger number of local opportunities accessible by public transport, are more likely to choose public transport for their commute (Box 2.4). The probability of taking public transport to go to work in Paris is, on average, 5 percentage points higher in a neighbourhood within the top 25% of neighbourhoods in terms of public transport performance than it is in the best performing neighbourhood among the bottom 25%.[7] For the metropolitan area of Marseille, the share of commuters between the same neighbourhoods differs but better performance only increases commute by 2 percentage points. Differences across cities in the extent to which transport uptake to commute to work is associated with the effectiveness of the public transport system depend on many factors, some of which are related to the public transport system, such as its cost, while some others depend on the characteristics of commuters (e.g. age, married status, number of kids, income, etc.).

Box 2.4. Does better public transport performance attract commuters in French metropolitan areas?

The probability that an individual living in a given area uses public transport to go to work as opposed to taking the car should be higher in areas where public transport offers better accessibility to local opportunities, i.e. where the public transport performance is high. Combining data on the share of workers who use public transport for their commute with performance indicators for different neighbourhoods of a sample of 11 French cities shows that this is generally the case, with better performing public transport drawing more travellers in large rather than small cities. "Performance" is defined as the percentage of opportunities (shops) within an 8 km radius that can be reached within a 30-minute ride by public transport from a given neighbourhood (500 m²-grid cell) within the metropolitan area.

Substantial differences emerge across French cities with respect to the capability of a better public transport system to attract a larger share of commuters. In Paris, for instance, a difference of 1 standard deviation in public transport performance (roughly comparing a neighbourhood at the 25th percentile with one at the 75th percentile in terms of public transport performance) is associated with a 5 percentage point higher share of commuters taking public transport. Given that the average commuter share across neighbourhoods in metropolitan Paris is about 31%, a 5 percentage point increase is a sizeable step up. In Marseille, only about 8% of workers take public transport in neighbourhoods with average public transport performance but the estimated benefit of going from the 25th to the 75th percentile of the public transport performance distribution in Marseille is only an increase of 2 percentage points. The probability of using public transport should also depend negatively on car performance. In Bordeaux, for instance, 3 percentage points more workers will choose public transport to go to work if public transport performance increases by 1 standard deviation but as many as 8 percentage points fewer workers will do so if car performance improves by 1 standard deviation.

Figure 2.6. Transport mode choice and transport performance in French cities, 2013

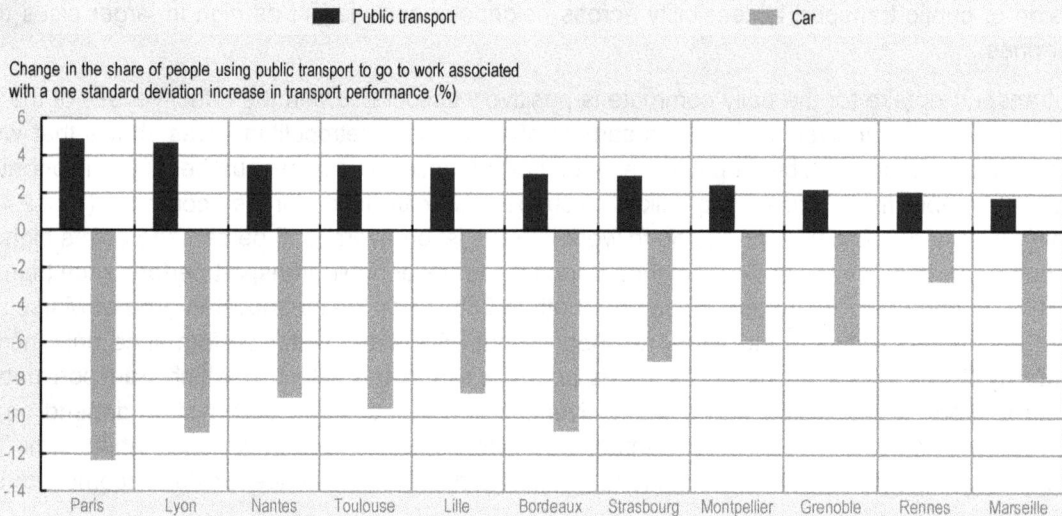

■ Public transport   ■ Car

Change in the share of people using public transport to go to work associated
with a one standard deviation increase in transport performance (%)

Paris Lyon Nantes Toulouse Lille Bordeaux Strasbourg Montpellier Grenoble Rennes Marseille

Note: Bars represent the coefficients of city-by-city linear regressions of the share (%) of people living in a given part of the city using public transport to go to work on the log difference between public transport performance (for 30 minutes and 8 km radius) from that part of the city and the city average, and similarly for car performance. Cities are sorted in descending order of the coefficient on public transport performance.
Source: Data on transport accessibility are from from ITF (2019[8]), *Benchmarking Accessibility in Cities*, International Transport Forum, Paris and INSEE (2019[19]), *Logement Ordinaire 2013*, https://www.insee.fr/fr/statistiques/2409491?sommaire=2409559 (accessed on 29 July 2019).

Richer neighbourhoods are characterised by better accessibility in three out of the four countries. In France, Italy and Spain, average accessibility in high-income neighbourhoods is much higher than in low-income neighbourhoods (Figure 2.7); in England, the opposite is the case for most metropolitan areas. Average accessibility in high-income neighbourhoods is on average 3 times higher than in low-income neighbourhoods in Italy for what concerns public transport. In France and Spain, the numbers are not very different respectively, 2.9 and 2.6. The city where inequality is the highest is Milan, the one where it is the lowest is Marseille, where public transport accessibility is nearly identical in high- and low-income neighbourhoods.

High-income residents in French, Italian and Spanish cities choose to live in neighbourhoods with better public transport accessibility. Time might be more valuable for high-income households that earn a higher hourly wage, thus increasing their willingness to pay higher housing costs in more accessible areas, in particular the city centre. Additionally, high-income residents tend to value more the proximity to amenities, such as restaurants, cinemas, cafés, which may disproportionately be located in the city centre (Diamond, 2016[20]).[8] There is also a tendency towards segregation of neighbourhoods by income levels that is stronger in more affluent, larger and more productive cities. The extent to which households concentrate in specific neighbourhoods tends to increase with their income levels (Patacchini et al., 2009[21]; OECD, 2018[22]).

Conversely, in England, high-income residents tend to have on average lower public transport accessibility than low-income ones. London and Sheffield are the only cities where high-income residents benefit from better accessibility than low-income ones but the differences are much smaller than for the other European cities in the sample. For instance, in London, accessibility in high-income neighbourhoods is just 27% higher than in low-income ones, which is a rather small number compared to the 500% in Milan. In all remaining English cities considered, public transport accessibility in high-income neighbourhoods is lower than in low-income ones. In Birmingham, for example, accessibility in high-income neighbourhoods is 16% of accessibility in low-income ones.

Figure 2.7. Low-income residents tend to live in areas with lower accessibility, 2018

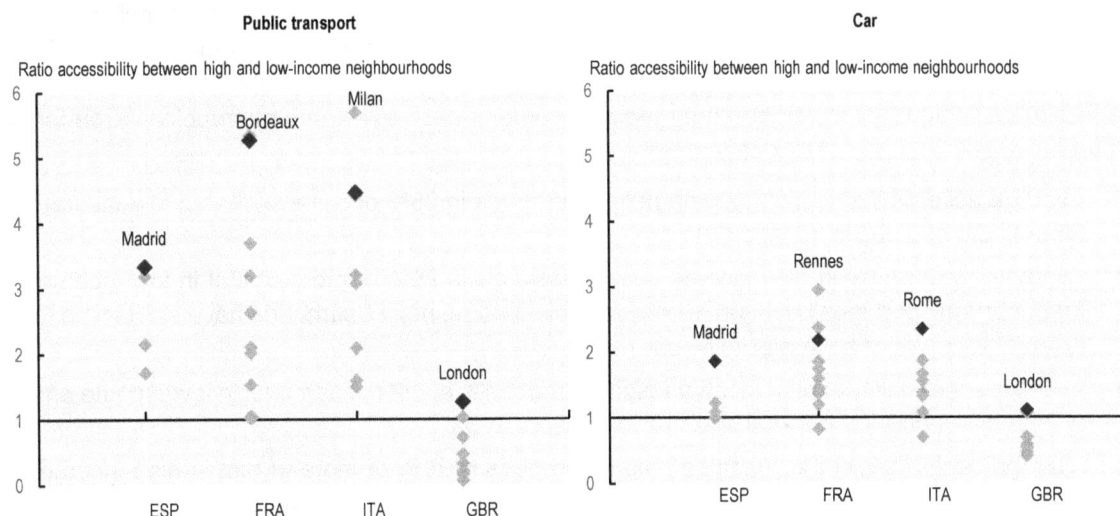

Note: Diamonds correspond to metropolitan areas with capital cities in the darker shade. Data for the United Kingdom includes only English metropolitan areas. On the vertical axis, the ratio between the population-weighted average accessibility in areas characterised by high income (above the city-specific 90th percentile of the income distribution) and the population-weighted average accessibility in areas characterised by low income (below the city-specific 10th percentile of the income distribution). Metropolitan areas with the highest ratio in each country are labelled. See Annex Table 2.A.3 for a description of income data.
Source: Data on transport accessibility are from ITF (2019[8]), *Benchmarking Accessibility in Cities*, International Transport Forum, Paris.

England's metropolitan areas are an exception because low-income residents disproportionately live in the centre of cities compared to metropolitan areas in France, Italy and Spain. English metropolitan areas share this characteristic with those in the United States (Glaeser, Kahn and Rappaport, 2008[23]). There are several potential explanations behind this empirical pattern. It can be, for instance, that richer households prefer to live in larger houses, thus purchasing a house in the suburbs where land is less scarce and housing costs per square metre are therefore lower. Alternatively, it can be that a private car is an expensive means of transport, while public transport is a cheap option, albeit more time-consuming, that is especially amenable to low-income residents. For this reason, low-income residents will sort into neighbourhoods characterised by better public transport accessibility, and hence the city centre.

Differences in housing policy can be responsible for the different residential patterns observed in European cities. Local and national governments efforts to keep housing affordable can substantially lift the opportunity for low-income households to enjoy higher levels of accessibility. Public instruments supporting housing affordability can be broadly classified into two groups: direct provision of social rental housing and housing costs subsidies, typically targeted towards low-income households and generally known as housing allowances. Countries differ widely in their policy mix: for instance, in Anglophone countries, social housing rental generally represents a rather low share of total dwellings, especially when compared against Northern European countries (Salvi Del Pero et al., 2015[24]). Among these countries, however, there are some, such as the United Kingdom, that spend a high share of their gross domestic product (GDP) in housing allowances.[9] It could be that housing costs subsidies by reducing the housing cost for low-income households in high-accessibility neighbourhoods favour a smaller accessibility gap between high- and low-income residents.

A snapshot of income and accessibility within (selected) metropolitan areas

In two-thirds of the 32 metropolitan areas considered, residents living in low-income neighbourhoods must rely on cars to get access to opportunities due to insufficient access via public transport. Furthermore, in half of the metropolitan areas, residents of low-income neighbourhoods have worse access to opportunities compared to residents in high-income neighbourhoods even when they rely on their car instead of public transport for getting around the city. In order to rank metropolitan areas in terms of inclusiveness in accessibility, average accessibility in high- and low-income neighbourhoods was computed. High- and low-income neighbourhoods in each metropolitan area are defined as those neighbourhoods where the average income is higher or lower than the median income in each city. Each metropolitan area for each transport mode falls into one of four categories:

1. Average accessibility in high-income neighbourhoods is 25% or more of that in low-income ones for both car and public transport trips.

2. Average accessibility in high-income neighbourhoods is 25% or more of that in low-income ones for public transport trips but high-income and low-income neighbourhoods have similar (up to 25% difference) levels of accessibility by car.

3. Average accessibility in high-income neighbourhoods is about the same as in low-income ones (up to 25% difference) for both car and public transport trips.

4. Average accessibility in low-income neighbourhoods is 25% or more of that in high-income ones for both car and public transport trips.

Categories	Examples
1. High-income neighbourhoods have better car and public transport accessibility	Bologna, Bordeaux, Firenze, Genova, Grenoble, Lille, Lyon, Madrid, Milano, Montpellier, Nantes, Paris, Rennes, Rome, Strasbourg, Toulouse
2. High-income neighbourhoods have better accessibility by public transport but not by car	Malaga, Napoli, Palermo, Torino, Valencia, Venezia
3. High- and low-income neighbourhoods have similar levels of accessibility	Bilbao, London, Marseille, Sheffield
4. Low-income neighbourhoods have better car and public transport access	Birmingham, Leeds, Leicester, Manchester, Newcastle, Nottingham

Table 2.2. *Cui bono?* **Accessibility for richer relative to poorer neighbourhoods in metropolitan areas**

Richer neighbourhoods have better car and public transport accessibility	Richer neighbourhoods have better accessibility by public transport but not by car	Richer and poorer neighbourhoods have similar levels of accessibility	Poorer neighbourhoods have better car and public transport access
Bologna	Malaga	Bilbao	Birmingham
Bordeaux	Naples	London	Leeds
Florence	Palermo	Marseille	Leicester
Genoa	Turin	Sheffield	Manchester
Grenoble	Valencia		Newcastle
Lille	Venice		Nottingham
Lyon			
Madrid			
Milan			
Montpellier			

	Nantes			
Paris			
Rennes			
Rome			
Strasbourg			
Toulouse			

Note: The threshold for "better" accessibility is at least 25% higher accessibility in one type of neighbourhood relative to the other, i.e. a large difference. Transport data refers to 2018 and income data to the closest year available. See Annex Table 2.A.3 for a description of income data. Source: Data on transport accessibility are from ITF (2019[8]), *Benchmarking Accessibility in Cities*, International Transport Forum, Paris.

One can identify two distinct degrees for the lack of inclusive access in metropolitan areas based on whether they feature a lack of inclusive access to just one or both. The first – and most severe – is one where a given metropolitan area lacks inclusive access with respect to both public transport and car. The second is milder than the first and identifies metropolitan areas that lack inclusive access only with respect to public transport. Despite public transport being a cheaper transport mode and therefore better suited for low-income households, in these cities, low-income residents could at least access the same number of opportunities as high-income ones if they relied on private cars. Equally importantly, no cities in the sample considered as a feature inclusive access to opportunities by public transport and not by car. This result can be a consequence of public transport accessibility being more heterogeneously distributed than car accessibility (Figure 2.5), thus implying that large differences between socio-economic groups are more likely to be detected for the first transport mode than the second one.

In one-third of the metropolitan areas, access to opportunities is inclusive, in the sense of low-income households enjoying at least as high accessibility as high-income ones. In 4 out of the 32 analysed metropolitan areas, access to opportunities is comparable between neighbourhoods above and below the median income. In six metropolitan areas, there is even a "reverse lack of inclusive access", in the sense of low-income households enjoying much higher levels of accessibility than high-income ones.

There is no systematic relationship between metropolitan areas providing good overall accessibility and whether accessibility is better for richer or poorer neighbourhoods. For example, London and Marseille provide equally good accessibility to both low- and high-income neighbourhoods. Nevertheless, average public transport accessibility (for both high- and low-income residents at this point) in London exceeds the one of Marseille by a factor of five.

A tale of four (types of) cities

High-income households have the best access in Rome

The centre of the metropolitan area of Rome in Italy is predominantly inhabited by high-income residents (Figure 2.8). Since public transport in the commuting zone is nearly absent or it has rather low performance, the public transport system in Rome clearly does not provide equal access to opportunities to all of Rome's residents. In particular, it is especially low-income households, disproportionately concentrated in the outskirts of the centre and the commuting zone, who must rely on private transport to access opportunities such as jobs or services.

The picture looks similar when focusing on car accessibility. There are some exceptions. One exception is, for instance, the southeast part of the commuting zone where the highway towards Naples and the Pontina – another important "fast road" connecting Rome with the industrial district on the way towards Latina – cuts across. Nevertheless, there remain large swathes of the commuting zone that suffer from low car accessibility, the result of which is the overall lack of inclusive access in the Italian capital with respect to private transport too.

Inclusive accessibility in Birmingham

Most metropolitan areas in England provide better accessibility to low-income neighbourhoods than high-income neighbourhoods. The location of households rather than the effectiveness of the transport system makes the difference compared to other metropolitan areas. In Birmingham, below-median income neighbourhoods are concentrated in and around the city centre. Households in these neighbourhoods, therefore, have access to a larger number of opportunities reachable either by public or private transport than high-income households (Figure 2.9). The high level of spending in housing allowances in the United Kingdom (1.06% over GDP in 2018 (OECD, 2020[25]) far above the OECD average of 0.26%) might be a contributor to the higher representation of low-income households in the centre of English cities, including Birmingham, compared to other countries.

Figure 2.8. Shops accessibility in Rome, 2018

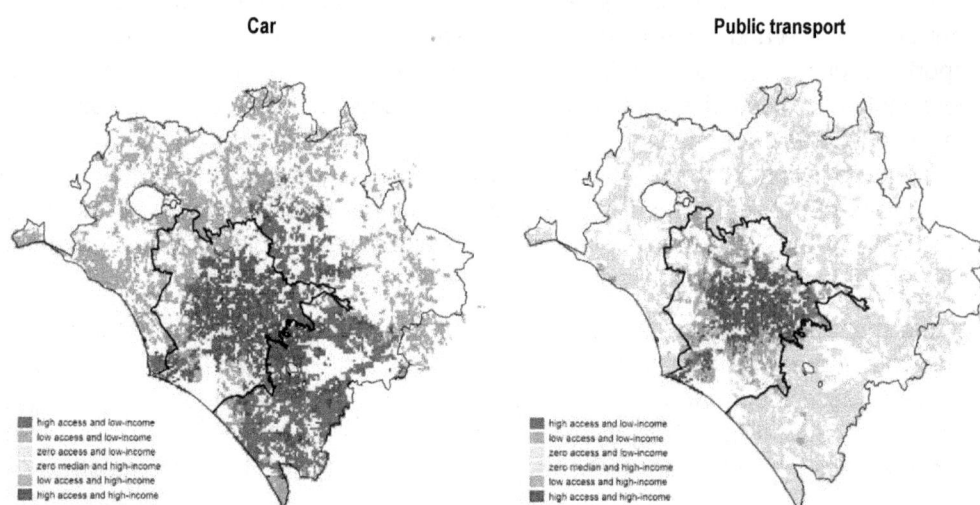

Note: Blue coloured cells correspond to cells with income below the city-specific median, where the median is population-weighted. Red coloured cells are those with income above. Darker coloured cells are those benefitting from better accessibility, light coloured one the opposite, where the threshold is given by the overall city-specific median. Outer boundaries denote the FUA, inner ones the core of the FUA. See Annex Table 2.A.3 for a description of income data.
Source: Data on transport accessibility are from ITF (2019[8]), *Benchmarking Accessibility in Cities*, International Transport Forum, Paris.

Figure 2.9. Shops accessibility in Birmingham, 2018

Car   Public transport

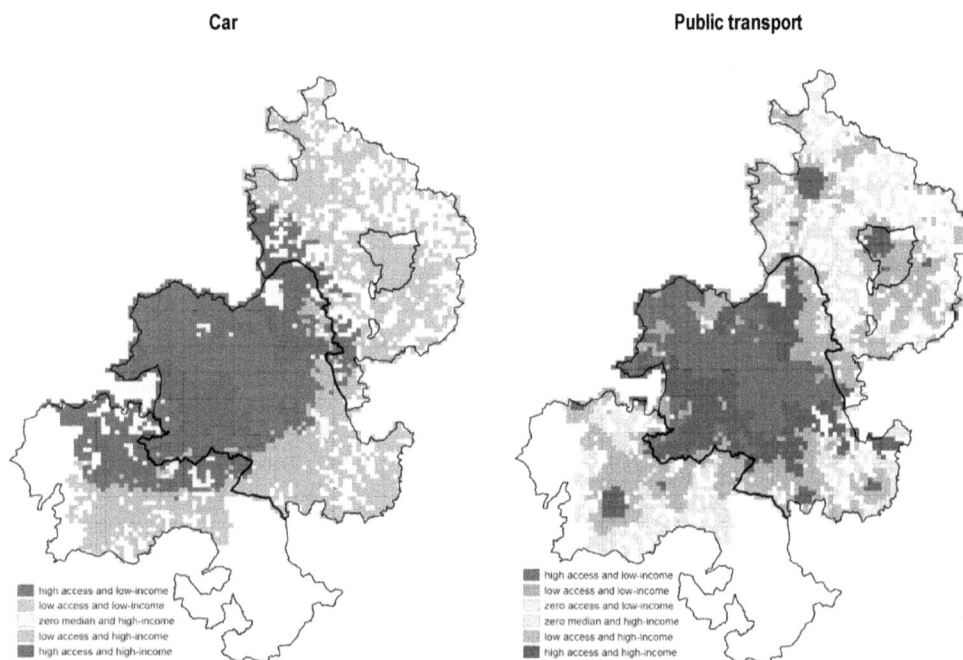

Note: Blue coloured cells correspond to cells with income below the city-specific median, where the median is population-weighted. Red coloured cells are those with income above. Darker coloured cells are those benefitting from better accessibility, light coloured one the opposite, where the threshold is given by the overall city-specific median. Outer boundaries denote the FUA, inner ones the core of the FUA. See Annex Table 2.A.3 for a description of income data.

Source: Data on transport accessibility are from ITF (2019[8]), *Benchmarking Accessibility in Cities*, International Transport Forum, Paris.

However, Birmingham has also one of the highest levels of income segregation among European metropolitan areas (OECD, 2018[22]). Low-income households are indeed very poorly mixed with people of a different socio-economic status. Housing allowances help low-income households afford to live in areas also inhabited by families with higher socio-economic status who might, however, choose to relocate elsewhere as low-income households' concentration increases. In the end, despite achieving greater housing affordability, high spending on housing allowances can run into the problem of fostering the transformation of certain areas of the city into enclaves inhabited predominantly by low-income households.

Housing policies aimed at expanding the access to social housing must be complemented by policies aimed at promoting "mixed communities" (Salvi Del Pero et al., 2015[24]). Mixed communities are characterised some degree by social diversity as opposed to social segregation. Housing segregation is associated with reduced upward mobility (Chetty and Hendren, 2018[26]) so that it is rarely an amenable outcome. While the principle of mixed communities for new housing development has represented an important tenet of English housing and planning policy since 2005 (Lupton and Fuller, 2009[27]), the higher degree of segregation in cities such as Birmingham or Manchester, as opposed to London for instance, shows that English cities have implemented it with a varying degree of success.

London is one of the few metropolitan areas with equal accessibility for different income groups

London differs from most other metropolitan areas in England as both low- and high-income residents enjoy a high degree of accessibility (Figure 2.10). As opposed to Birmingham, social segregation is lower, a sign that housing policies geared towards the preservation of "mixed communities" have been more successful in the British capital than in other metropolitan areas in England.

Figure 2.10. Shops accessibility in London, 2018

Car   Public transport

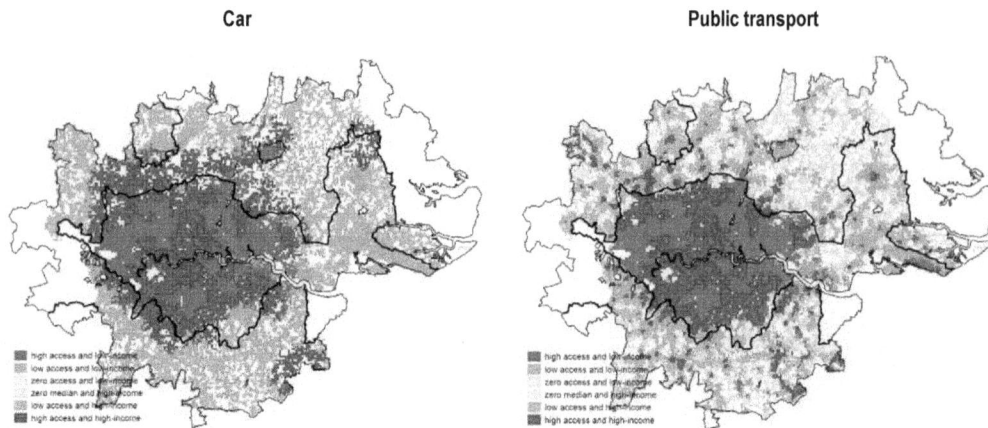

Note: Blue coloured cells correspond to cells with income below the city-specific median, where the median is population-weighted. Red coloured cells are those with income above. Darker coloured cells are those benefitting from better accessibility, light coloured one the opposite, where the threshold is given by the overall city-specific median. Outer boundaries denote the FUA, inner ones the core of the FUA. See Annex Table 2.A.3 for a description of income data.
Source: Data on transport accessibility are from ITF (2019[8]), *Benchmarking Accessibility in Cities*, International Transport Forum, Paris.

The commuting zone also benefits from high accessibility thanks to a dense public transport network that stretches well out into the commuting zone. Public transport stops are identifiable on the map by means of the dark dots aligned along the radii departing from the city centre. High density (and proximity of opportunities) at the train stations located in the commuting zone is achieved thanks to tight co-ordination with regulators in charge of disciplining land-use and developers. For instance, the fact that the London transport authority (Transport for London or TfL) also owns much of the land surrounding the train stations favours property development around them thus raising the range of opportunities accessible in the commuting zone given the transport network.[10]

Public transport in Paris favours the urban centre

Nine out of ten French metropolitan areas feature a severe lack of inclusive access to opportunities. Paris, the French capital, is one such example. The comparison between Paris (Figure 2.11) and London offers an example of how land-use patterns can affect accessibility. The Parisian commuting zone – where 22% of the total population of the metropolitan area live – is characterised by a low degree of accessibility around public transport stops compared to London. It is easy to pinpoint on the map where stations of the commuter trains (e.g. RER, Transilien) are located: both cities feature sequences of high-accessibility hotspots in the commuting zone located along with a set of radii departing from the city centre. However, higher accessibility in Paris is limited to a much more geographically limited neighbourhood around public transport stops compared to London.

Figure 2.11. Shops accessibility in Paris, 2018

Car   Public transport

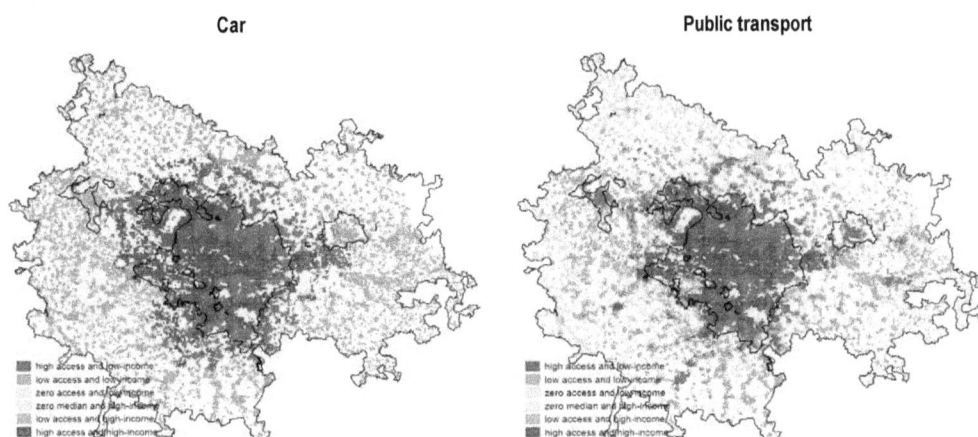

Note: Blue coloured cells correspond to cells with income below the city-specific median, where the median is population-weighted. Red coloured cells are those with income above. Darker coloured cells are those benefitting from better accessibility, light coloured one the opposite, where the threshold is given by the overall city-specific median. Outer boundaries denote the FUA, inner ones the core of the FUA. See Annex Table 2.A.3 for a description of income data.
Source: Data on transport accessibility are from ITF (2019[8]), *Benchmarking Accessibility in Cities*, International Transport Forum, Paris.

Hence, the articulated public transport network that stretches well into the commuting zone in both cities provides access to fewer opportunities for Parisians than it does for Londoners. A likely explanation for the different pattern is the limited availability of opportunities in the proximity of public transport stops in Paris, which stands in great contrast with the traditional service-rich high streets in many London boroughs, including peripheral ones (Carmona, 2015[28]). The disproportionate concentration of services and economic activity at large in the city centre is a long-standing feature of the French capital. The *villes nouvelles* strategy elaborated in the 1960s aimed at addressing what was then perceived as a barrier to growth and decentralising economic activity in a few large French cities, including Paris. Besides the creation of new towns around delocalised production centres in the commuting zone of the city, the new strategy included the construction of the RER public transport network, with the objective of integrating the new different local labour markets. Ensuring mixed development and therefore homogenous access to services besides jobs along these newly formed public transport axes was not a declared priority at that time. It is, however, an objective of the Grand Paris Express, an important project – currently under construction – that aims at better integrating via public transport the Parisian commuting zone, also known as the *couronne Parisienne* (Beaucire and Drevelle, 2013[29]).

Low-income households in Valencia need to rely on cars for accessibility, high-income households benefit from public transport

Residents in low-income neighbourhoods in about 20% of metropolitan areas have at least as good accessibility as high-income neighbourhoods, but only by car. Low-income neighbourhoods in Valencia (Figure 2.12) are clustered in the immediate periphery around the city centre and the southern commuting zone at large. In contrast, high-income neighbourhoods tend to be concentrated either in the city centre or in the northern commuting zone. Despite the coastal highway running all around the commuting zone, car accessibility in the northern part is less than in the south owing to the mountainous terrain and lower residential development intensity. For this reason, low-income households can access a similar number of opportunities by car to one of high-income residents, in spite of having reduced access to the services-rich city centre. Conversely, the concentration of high-income residents in the city centre is responsible for a rather low degree of inclusiveness in public transport accessibility.

Figure 2.12. Shops accessibility in Valencia, 2018

Car   Public transport

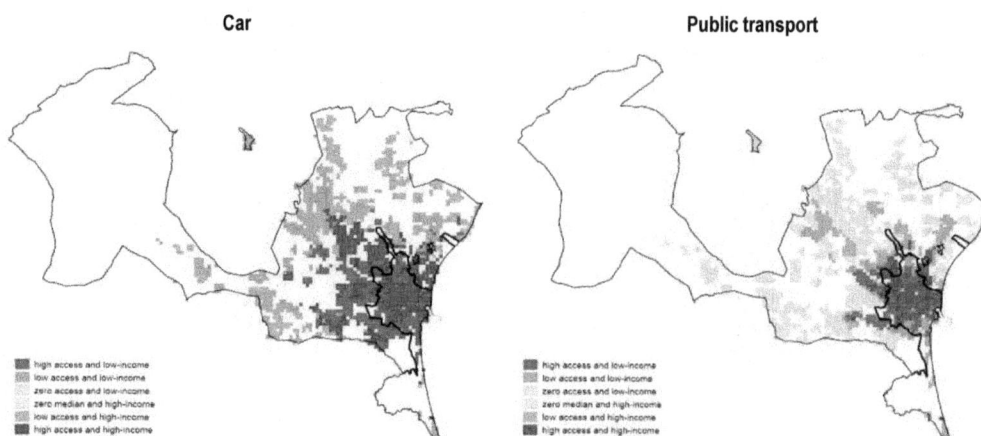

Note: Blue coloured cells correspond to cells with income below the city-specific median, where the median is population-weighted. Red coloured cells are those with income above. Darker coloured cells are those benefitting from better accessibility, light coloured one the opposite, where the threshold is given by the overall city-specific median. Outer boundaries denote the FUA, inner ones the core of the FUA. See Annex Table 2.A.3 for a description of income data.
Source: Data on transport accessibility are from ITF (2019[8]), *Benchmarking Accessibility in Cities*, International Transport Forum, Paris.

A snapshot of income and accessibility across (selected) metropolitan areas

Differences in accessibility between high- and low-income neighbourhoods depend on where people live within a metropolitan area but also in what metropolitan area they choose to live. Differences in the sorting pattern of high- compared to low-income residents across cities are just as marked as differences in the sorting pattern within cities. Residents in larger cities tend to be, on average, better educated and have higher income levels than residents of smaller cities (OECD, 2015[30]). As larger cities offer better accessibility on average across their neighbourhoods (Figure 2.3), differences in the way high- and low-income households sort across cities constitutes an additional factor driving overall differences in accessibility between income groups. As a result, high-income residents benefit from better accessibility not only because they live in parts of the metropolitan area where access to opportunities is on average better (Figure 2.7) but also because many of them live in richer metropolitan areas that enjoy overall better access to opportunities, regardless of the location within the city.

In France, for example, Parisians account for 85% of people who live in the richest top 10% of neighbourhoods across the 11 metropolitan areas considered. This share rises to 100% in the top-income percentiles. In contrast, (as good as) none of the top-income neighbourhoods can be found in Lille, the capital of France's northernmost region Hauts-de-France. Lille and Paris are also the two metropolitan areas where the number of shops accessible within 30 minutes of public transport is respectively the lowest and the highest (Figure 2.3).

Metropolitan areas in England tend to provide inclusive access but, across metropolitan areas, there are dramatic differences in where the richest and the poorest part of the population live. All neighbourhoods in the top 10% of the income distribution are in London, the metropolitan area with highest public transport accessibility, on average. In contrast, none of the top 25% of neighbourhoods in terms of household income can be found in Birmingham (Figure 2.3), the metropolitan area with the lowest level of public transport accessibility, about 1/20th of London's.[11]

Figure 2.13. High-income households are more likely to live in high-accessibility cities in France and England, 2018

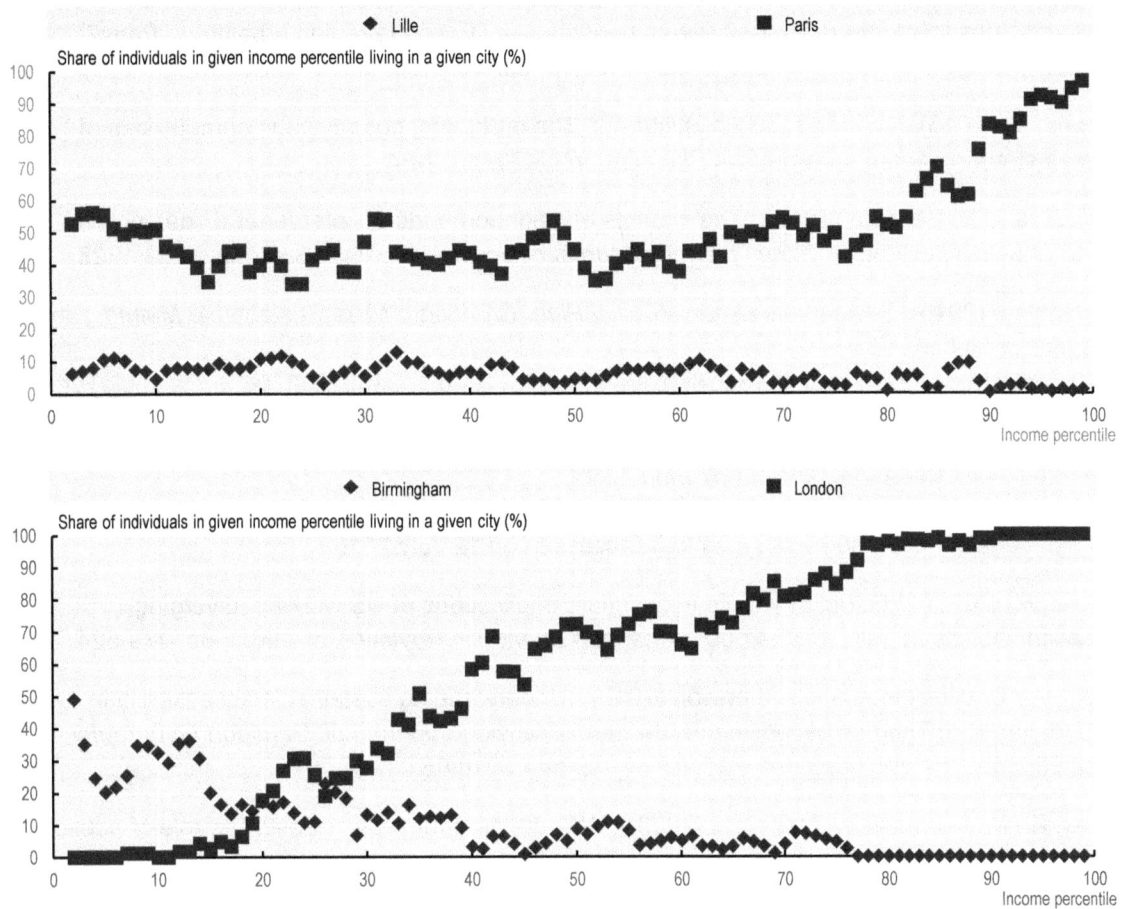

Note: Each dot corresponds to a percentile of the aggregate income distribution in the country. On the vertical axis, a moving average (-1,+1) centred on the percentile of reference of the share of individuals belonging to that income percentile and living in a given city is plotted. See Annex Table 2.A.3 for a description of income data.

References

Beaucire, F. and M. Drevelle (2013), "«Grand Paris Express» : un projet au service de la réduction des inégalités d'accessibilité entre l'Ouest et l'Est de la région urbaine de Paris?", *Revue d'Économie Régionale and Urbaine*, Vol. 3, pp. 437-460. [29]

Carmona, M. (2015), "London's local high streets: The problems, potential and complexities of mixed street corridors", *Progress in Planning*, Vol. 100, pp. 1-84. [28]

Chetty, R. and N. Hendren (2018), "The impacts of neighborhoods on intergenerational mobility II: County-level estimates", *The Quarterly Journal of Economics*, Vol. 133/3, pp. 1163-1228. [26]

City of Malmö (2016), *Sustainable Urban Mobility Plan: Creating a More Sustainable Malmö*, City Council of Malmö, https://malmo.se/download/18.16ac037b154961d0287384d/1491301288704/Sustainable+urban+mobility+plan%28TROMP%29_ENG.pdf (accessed on 16 July 2019). [13]

City of Stockholm (n.d.), *Stockholm City Plan*, https://vaxer.stockholm/globalassets/tema/oversiktplan-ny_light/english_stockholm_city_plan.pdf (accessed on 12 July 2019). [12]

Diamond, R. (2016), "The determinants and welfare implications of US workers' diverging location choices by skill: 1980–2000", *American Economic Review*, Vol. 106/3, pp. 479-524. [20]

Gil Solá, A., B. Vilhelmson and A. Larsson (2018), "Understanding sustainable accessibility in urban planning: Themes of consensus, themes of tension", *Journal of Transport Geography*, Vol. 70, pp. 1-10, http://dx.doi.org/10.1016/j.jtrangeo.2018.05.010. [10]

Glaeser, E., M. Kahn and J. Rappaport (2008), "Why do the poor live in cities? The role of public transportation", *Journal of Urban Economics*, Vol. 63/1, pp. 1-24. [23]

Greater London Authority (2018), *Mayor's Transport Strategy*, http://www.london.gov.uk (accessed on 15 July 2019). [5]

Hellberg, S. et al. (2014), *Gothenburg 2035 - Transport Strategy for a Close-Knit City*, Urban Transport Committee, City of Gothenburg, https://goteborg.se/wps/wcm/connect/6c603463-f0b8-4fc9-9cd4-c1e934b41969/Trafikstrategi_eng_140821_web.pdf?MOD=AJPERES (accessed on 16 July 2019). [11]

INSEE (2019), *Logement Ordinaire 2013*, https://www.insee.fr/fr/statistiques/2409491?sommaire=2409559 (accessed on 29 17 2019). [19]

IPCC (2014), "Transport", in *Climate Change 2014: Mitigation of Climate Change. Contribution of Working Group III to the Fifth Assessment Report of the Intergovernmental Panel on Climate Change*, Intergovernmental Panel on Climate Change, Postdam, https://www.ipcc.ch/site/assets/uploads/2018/02/ipcc_wg3_ar5_chapter8.pdf (accessed on 17 July 2019). [15]

ITF (2020), "Re-spacing Our Cities For Resilience", International Transport Forum, Paris, https://www.itf-oecd.org/sites/default/files/respacing-cities-resilience-covid-19.pdf (accessed on 3 June 2020). [16]

ITF (2019), *Benchmarking Accessibility in Cities*, International Transport Forum, Paris. [8]

ITF (2019), *Improving Transport Planning and Investment Through the Use of Accessibility Indicators*, International Transport Forum, Paris, http://www.itf-oecd.org (accessed on 16 July 2019). [9]

Leinberger, C. and M. Alfonzo (2012), *Walk this Way: The Economic Promise of Walkable Places in Metropolitan Washington, D.C.*. [3]

Litman, T. (2015), *Analysis of Public Policies That Unintentionally Encourage and Subsidize Urban Sprawl*, The New Climate Economy. [2]

Lupton, R. and C. Fuller (2009), "Mixed communities: A new approach to spatially concentrated poverty in England", *International Journal of Urban and Regional Research*, Vol. 33/4, pp. 1014-1028. [27]

NYC DOT (2016), *New York City Strategic Plan 2016*, Department of Transportation, New York, https://www.nycdotplan.nyc/PDF/Strategic-plan-2016.pdf (accessed on 6 August 2019). [4]

OECD (2020), *A Territorial Approach to the Sustainable Development Goals: Synthesis report*, OECD Urban Policy Reviews, OECD Publishing, Paris, https://doi.org/10.1787/e86fa715-en. [6]

OECD (2020), *Affordable Housing Database*, OECD, Paris, http://www.oecd.org/social/affordable-housing-database/housing-policies/. [25]

OECD (2018), *Divided Cities: Understanding Intra-urban Inequalities*, OECD Publishing Paris, https://doi.org/10.1787/9789264300385-en. [22]

OECD (2017), *Urban Transport Governance and Inclusive Development in Korea*, OECD Publishing, Paris, https://dx.doi.org/10.1787/9789264272637-en. [17]

OECD (2016), *Road Infrastructure, Inclusive Development and Traffic Safety in Korea*, OECD Publishing, Paris, https://dx.doi.org/10.1787/9789264255517-en. [7]

OECD (2015), *OECD Territorial Reviews: Valle de México, Mexico*, OECD Territorial Reviews, OECD Publishing, Paris, https://doi.org/10.1787/9789264245174-en. [1]

OECD (2015), *The Metropolitan Century: Understanding Urbanisation and its Consequences*, OECD Publishing, Paris, https://doi.org/10.1787/9789264228733-en. [30]

Patacchini, E. et al. (2009), *Urban Sprawl in Europe*. [21]

Rode, P. et al. (2014), "Accessibility in cities: Transport and urban form", *NCE Cities Paper 03*, LSE Cities, London School of Economics and Political Science, http://www.lsecities.net (accessed on 9 July 2019). [14]

Salvi Del Pero, A. et al. (2015), "Policies to promote access to good-quality affordable housing in OECD countries", *OECD Social, Employment and Migration Working Papers*, No. 176, OECD Publishing, Paris, https://doi.org/10.1787/5jm3p5gl4djd-en. [24]

Swinney, P. and E. Bidgood (2014), "Fast track to growth transport priorities for stronger cities". [18]

Notes

[1] See Chapter 1 for a review of the positive externalities associated with density.

[2] The average number of shops accessible within 30 minutes in the 20 largest metropolitan areas in the sample is 3.2 times the number in the smallest 20 cities for access by car and 2.8 times for public transport. The largest metropolitan areas have at least 2 million inhabitants for public transport and 2.6 million for access by car. The smallest 20 range from 420 000 inhabitants to 750 000 (public transport) or 625 000 (car).

[3] See Annex Figure 2.A.1 and Annex Figure 2.A.2 for access to schools and hospitals.

[4] Access to shops proxies for access to jobs that are more concentrated than population. Calculating the difference in access to people rather than shops shows a smaller (albeit still sizeable) disadvantage of living in the commuting zone (ITF, 2019[9]). The difference reflects the concentration of jobs (and shops) in city centres.

[5] The difference is calculated as $difference = 100 \times 2(p(75) - p(25))/(p(75) + p(25))$, which allows to retain metropolitan areas for which the 25th percentile of the accessibility distribution is equal to 0. The calculated difference ranges from 0 to 200 with small values coinciding with the percent difference between the percentiles. For large values the stated numbers are rescaled to percent differences. Concretely 150 corresponds to about 670% and 85% to 250%.

[6] The smallest metropolitan areas correspond to the 12 (10% of the sample) smallest ones in the sample with 414 000 to 565 000 inhabitants and the largest 12 metropolitan areas are those with 3 million to 12 million inhabitants. A difference of 60 corresponds to about 185% difference in accessibility and a difference of 116% to 380%. See also the preceding endnote.

[7] Neighbourhoods are grid cells (500 m²) and the comparison refers to the 75th percentile neighbourhood compared to the 25th percentile.

[8] There is evidence that one of the reasons behind the divergence in residential choices of high-skilled and low-skilled people that led to the increasing concentration of the first group in a small set of US cities between 1980 and 2000 has been the capability of these cities to develop an attractive offer of amenities geared towards them (Diamond, 2016[20]).

[9] In the United Kingdom, total spending on housing allowances amounted to 1.06% over GDP in 2018, far above the OECD average of 0.26% (OECD, 2020[25]).

[10] TfL owned 5 700 acres of land in 2015 in the Greater London area. However, this number includes also land that cannot be used for building on because occupied by railways or roads. See https://www.theguardian.com/uk-news/davehillblog/2015/oct/20/transport-for-london-picks-first-300-acres-for-property-development-drive.

[11] These percentiles refer to the distribution obtained pooling together the metropolitan areas considered in this report. Such distribution abstracts therefore from earnings of individuals living outside of these metropolitan areas. The units considered to calculate this distribution are Lower Super Output Areas, which contain an average of 1 500 individuals.

Annex 2.A. Data sources and additional figures

Accessibility data

The EC-ITF-OECD Urban Access Framework has been implemented for 121 functional urban areas (FUAs). The car accessibility indicators discussed in this chapter refer to 118 FUAs from 25 European OECD countries and 2 European Union, non-OECD member countries. Public transport accessibility indicators are available for a subset of cities, 82 in total.

Annex Table 2.A.1. FUAs with available car accessibility estimates

Name	FUA code	Name	FUA code	Name	FUA code
Vienna	AT001	Thessaloniki	EL002	Riga	LV001
Graz	AT002	Madrid	ES001	The Hague	NL001
Linz	AT003	Barcelona	ES002	Amsterdam	NL002
Brussels	BE001	Valencia	ES003	Rotterdam	NL003
Antwerp	BE002	Seville	ES004	Utrecht	NL004
Gent	BE003	Saragossa	ES005	Eindhoven	NL005
Liege	BE005	Malaga	ES006	Oslo	NO001
Sofia	BG001	Las Palmas	ES008	Warsaw	PL001
Plovdiv	BG002	Bilbao	ES019	Lodz	PL002
Varna	BG003	Helsinki	FI001	Cracow	PL003
Zurich	CH001	Paris	FR001	Wroclaw	PL004
Geneva	CH002	Lyon	FR003	Poznan	PL005
Basel	CH003	Toulouse	FR004	Gdansk	PL006
Prague	CZ001	Strasbourg	FR006	Lublin	PL009
Brno	CZ002	Bordeaux	FR007	Katowice	PL010
Ostrava	CZ003	Nantes	FR008	Lisbon	PT001
Berlin	DE001	Lille	FR009	Porto	PT002
Hamburg	DE002	Montpellier	FR010	Bucaresti	RO001
Munich	DE003	Saint-Etienne	FR011	Stockholm	SE001
Cologne	DE004	Rennes	FR013	Gothenburg	SE002
Frankfurt am Main	DE005	Grenoble	FR026	Malmö	SE003
Stuttgart	DE007	Toulon	FR032	Ljubljana	SI001
Leipzig	DE008	Marseille	FR203	Bratislava	SK001
Dresden	DE009	Nice	FR205	London	UK001
Dusseldorf	DE011	Rouen	FR215	West Midlands urban area	UK002
Bremen	DE012	Budapest	HU001	Leeds	UK003
Hanover	DE013	Dublin	IE001	Glasgow	UK004
Nuremberg	DE014	Rome	IT001	Liverpool	UK006
Freiburg im Breisgau	DE027	Milan	IT002	Edinburgh	UK007
Augsburg	DE033	Naples	IT003	Manchester	UK008
Bonn	DE034	Turin	IT004	Cardiff	UK009
Karlsruhe	DE035	Palermo	IT005	Sheffield	UK010

Name	FUA code	Name	FUA code	Name	FUA code
Ruhr	DE038	Genoa	IT006	Bristol	UK011
Saarbrucken	DE040	Florence	IT007	Belfast	UK012
Mannheim-Ludwigshafen	DE084	Bari	IT008	Newcastle upon Tyne	UK013
Muenster	DE504	Bologna	IT009	Leicester	UK014
Aachen	DE507	Catania	IT010	Portsmouth	UK023
Copenhagen	DK001	Venice	IT011	Nottingham	UK029
Tallinn	EE001	Vilnius	LT001		
Athens	EL001	Luxembourg	LU001		

Source: Data on transport accessibility are from ITF (2019[8]), *Benchmarking Accessibility in Cities*, International Transport Forum, Paris.

Annex Table 2.A.2. FUAs with available public transport accessibility estimates

Name	FUA code	Name	FUA code	Name	FUA code
Vienna	AT001	Lyon	FR003	Utrecht	NL004
Brussels	BE001	Toulouse	FR004	Eindhoven	NL005
Antwerp	BE002	Strasbourg	FR006	Oslo	NO001
Gent	BE003	Bordeaux	FR007	Warsaw	PL001
Liege	BE005	Nantes	FR008	Wroclaw	PL004
Zurich	CH001	Lille	FR009	Gdansk	PL006
Geneva	CH002	Montpellier	FR010	Lisbon	PT001
Basel	CH003	Rennes	FR013	Stockholm	SE001
Prague	CZ001	Grenoble	FR026	Gothenburg	SE002
Berlin	DE001	Marseille	FR203	Malmö	SE003
Hamburg	DE002	Nice	FR205	Ljubljana	SI001
Cologne	DE004	Budapest	HU001	London	UK001
Leipzig	DE008	Dublin	IE001	West Midlands urban area	UK002
Nuremberg	DE014	Rome	IT001	Leeds	UK003
Bonn	DE034	Milan	IT002	Glasgow	UK004
Karlsruhe	DE035	Naples	IT003	Liverpool	UK006
Mannheim-Ludwigshafen	DE084	Turin	IT004	Edinburgh	UK007
Aachen	DE507	Palermo	IT005	Manchester	UK008
Copenhagen	DK001	Genoa	IT006	Cardiff	UK009
Tallinn	EE001	Florence	IT007	Sheffield	UK010
Athens	EL001	Bologna	IT009	Bristol	UK011
Madrid	ES001	Venice	IT011	Belfast	UK012
Valencia	ES003	Vilnius	LT001	Newcastle upon Tyne	UK013
Malaga	ES006	Luxembourg	LU001	Leicester	UK014
Las Palmas	ES008	Riga	LV001	Portsmouth	UK023
Bilbao	ES019	The Hague	NL001	Nottingham	UK029
Helsinki	FI001	Amsterdam	NL002		
Paris	FR001	Rotterdam	NL003		

Source: Data on transport accessibility are from ITF (2019[8]), *Benchmarking Accessibility in Cities*, International Transport Forum, Paris.

Income data

Not all countries provide data on income (or proxies thereof) at a highly disaggregated level, such as the neighbourhood level. The analysis on the distribution of accessibility across neighbourhoods according to their socio-economic status has been carried out on a sample of four large European countries that do, i.e. England (UK), France, Italy and Spain. The variables used to measure or proxy for income and the corresponding data sources are provided in Annex Table 2.A.3.

To link accessibility data with income levels, a 500-by-500-metre grid is overlapped with census tracts boundaries containing sociodemographic information. Sociodemographic information is then assigned at the grid cell level by taking a weighted average of the income variable (or its proxy) across overlapping census tracts. Only grids with no missing information for both income and accessibility and strictly positive population are retained.

Annex Table 2.A.3. Disaggregated data sources on income or proxies thereof

Variable	Geography level	Source	Link
Disposable income	Middle Layer Super Output Areas	ONS	https://www.ons.gov.uk/employmentandlabourmarket/peoplei nwork/earningsandworkinghours/datasets/smallareaincomees timatesformiddlelayersuperoutputareasenglandandwales
Share of employment professional/ managerial occupations	IRIS	INSEE	https://www.insee.fr/fr/statistiques?taille=100&debut=0&idprec =2386703&categorie=3&geo=ICQ-1
Share with tertiary education	Sezioni di censimento	ISTAT	https://www.istat.it/it/archivio/104317
Share with tertiary education	Secciones censales	INE	http://www.ine.es/censos2011_datos/cen11_datos_resultados _seccen.htm

Accessibility of schools and hospitals

Annex Figure 2.A.1. Number of schools accessible within a 30-minute ride, 2018

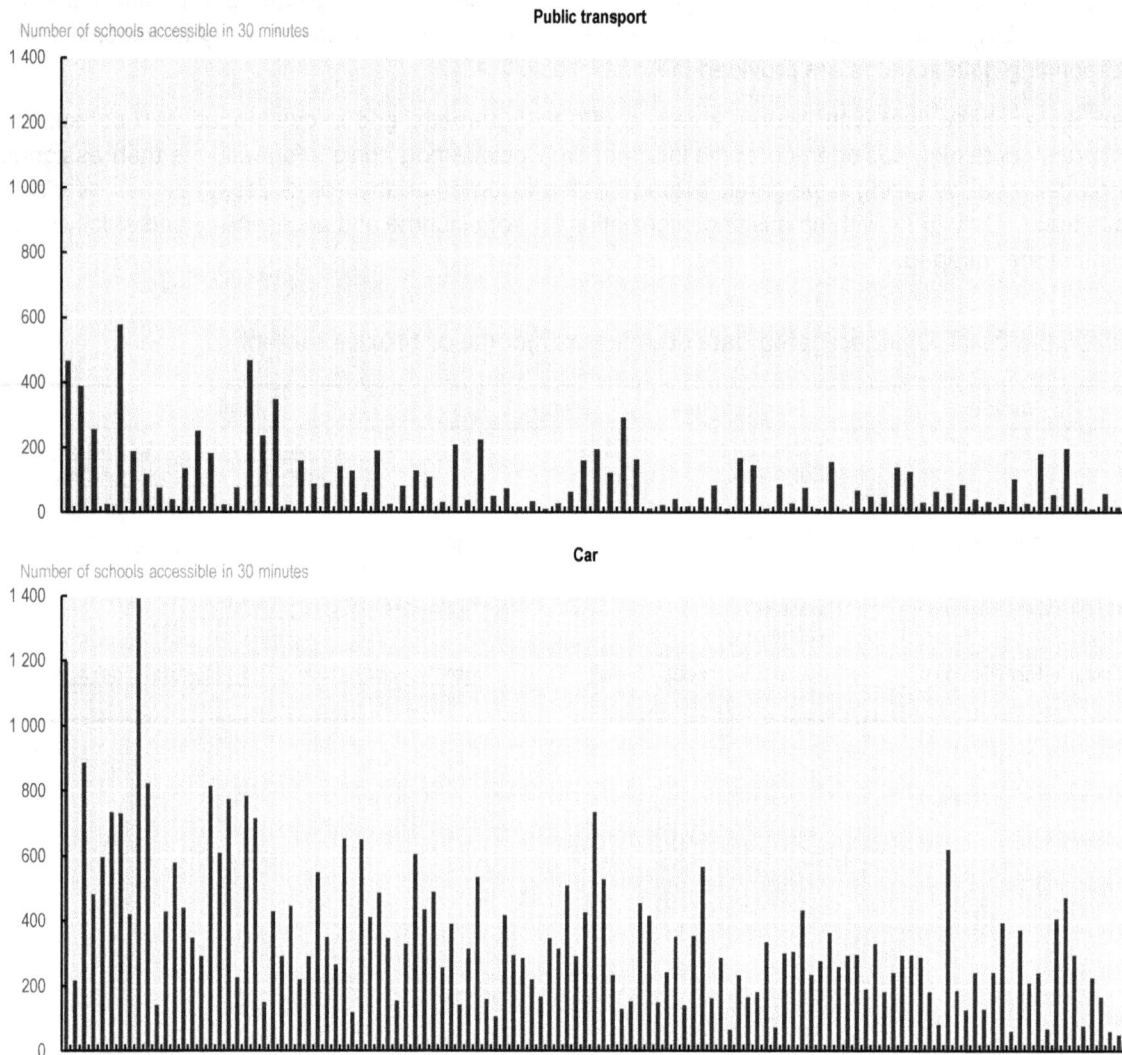

Public transport

Number of schools accessible in 30 minutes

Car

Number of schools accessible in 30 minutes

Note: Each bar corresponds to an FUA or city. The length of each bar corresponds to the average number of schools accessible within a 30-minute ride by public transport (upper panel) or by car (lower panel). Cities are sorted in descending order according to their total population. Average accessibility per city is calculated as a weighted average of cell-specific accessibility with weights given by the population residing in a cell relative to the total population. 118 metropolitan areas for car accessibility and 82 for public transport accessibility.

Source: Data on transport accessibility are from ITF (2019[8]), *Benchmarking Accessibility in Cities*, International Transport Forum, Paris.

Annex Figure 2.A.2. Number of hospitals accessible within a 30-minute ride, 2018

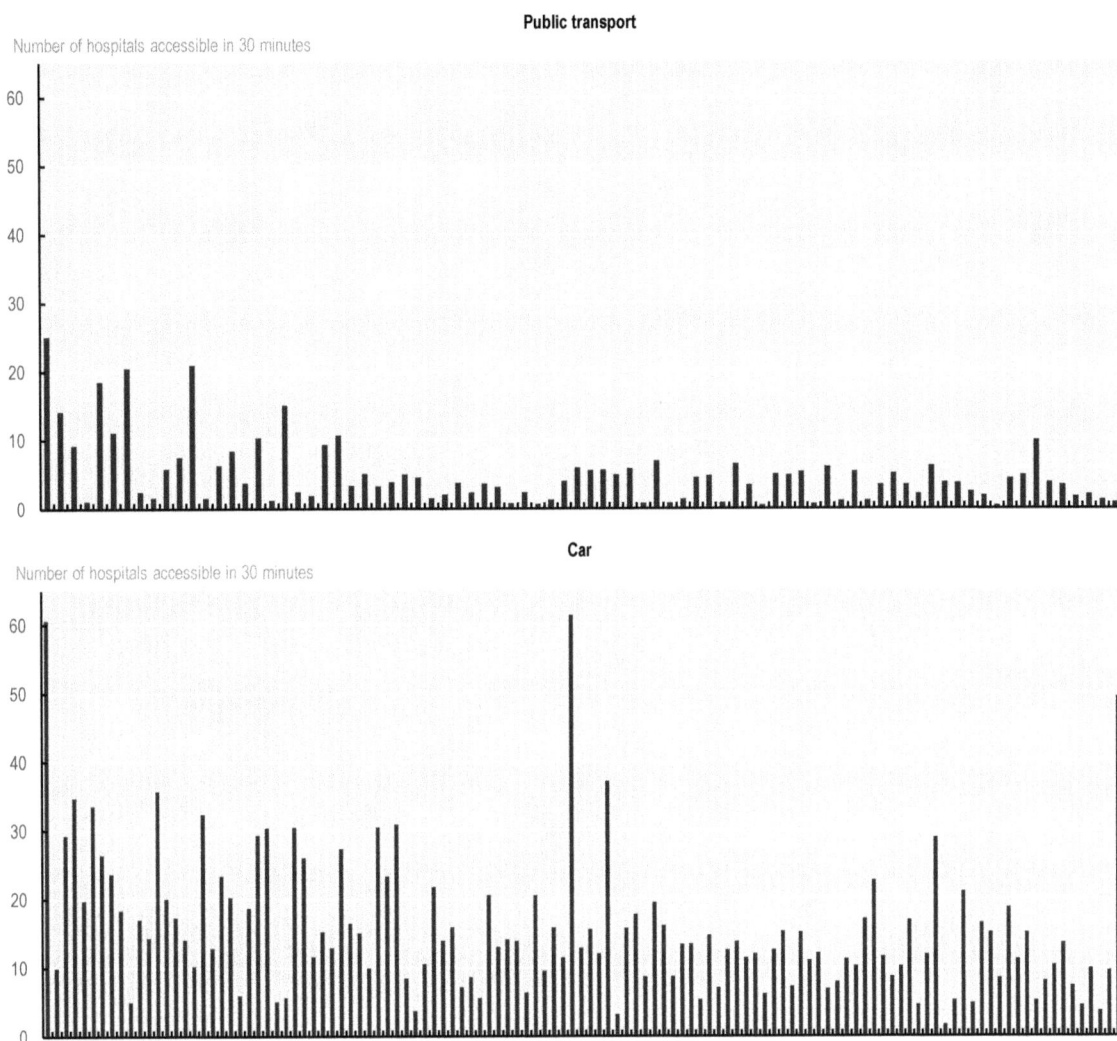

Public transport

Number of hospitals accessible in 30 minutes

Car

Number of hospitals accessible in 30 minutes

Note: Each bar corresponds to a FUA or city. The length of each bar corresponds to the average number of hospitals accessible within a 30-minute ride by public transport (upper panel) or by car (lower panel). Cities are sorted in descending order according to their total population. Average accessibility per city is calculated as a weighted average of cell-specific accessibility with weights given by the population residing in a cell relative to the total population. 118 metropolitan areas for car accessibility and 82 for public transport accessibility. Source: Data on transport accessibility are from the International Transport Forum (2019[8]).

www.ingramcontent.com/pod-product-compliance
Lightning Source LLC
Chambersburg PA
CBHW080339270326
41927CB00014B/3293